D1435237

OG DAD

8/6/15

Mark a box below with your initials or a symbol if you
wish a reminder that you have read this book.

JERRY STAHL

OG DAD

Weird Shit Happens When You Don't Die Young

THIS IS A GENUINE RARE BIRD BOOK

A Rare Bird Book | Rare Bird Books
453 South Spring Street, Suite 302
Los Angeles, CA 90013
rarebirdbooks.com

FIRST TRADE PAPERBACK ORIGINAL EDITION

Set in Minion
Printed in the United States

10 9 8 7 6 5 4 3 2 1

Publisher's Cataloging-in-Publication data

Stahl, Jerry.
    Old guy dad : weird shit happens when you don't die young / by
Jerry Stahl.
    p. cm.
    ISBN 978-0988745629

1. Stahl, Jerry. 2. Fathers—Biography. 3. Middle-aged fathers—
Biography. 4. Children of older parents. 5. Parent and child. I. Title.

HQ756 .S735 2015
306.874/2/0844—dc23

For Elizabeth, Stella, & Nico

"To be the father of growing daughters is to understand something of what Yeats evokes with his imperishable phrase 'terrible beauty.' Nothing can make one so happily exhilarated or so frightened: it's a solid lesson in the limitations of self to realize that your heart is running around inside someone else's body. It also makes me quite astonishingly calm at the thought of death: I know whom I would die to protect and I also understand that nobody but a lugubrious serf can possibly wish for a father who never goes away."

—Christopher Hitchens

INTROD

UCTION

WHEN I IMAGINE THE future, I see my daughter clawing her way across a blistered landscape, gasping for water, grubbing for cancer scraps while struggling to endure five more minutes in some world stripped of sustenance by the greed and idiocy of the generation that raped it to the bone before hers ever had a chance... I'm dead by then, but even from beyond the grave I feel guilty for having brought her into the living hell of the Monsanto-ravaged, Boko-Haramed, Naomi Klein dystopia that's in the mail.

This, in our current era, is the peculiar thrill of spawning a child when you're no longer young: along with the joy of looming mortality, there's the festive knowledge that you and the planet are both already seventy-five percent dead before the tyke even rolls in.

But maybe I'm being optimistic. I can't speak for other post-fifty fathers, but I feel like these are my pre-tumor years, my avant-stroke time, to be enjoyed until the moment my heart stops beating and starts attacking. Throw a toddler in the mix and you've got an unnatural, if thrill-packed and delightful, setup for decline.

(I should add, I was more or less dying when the baby was conceived; at the tail end of a twenty-year run of needle-induced hepatitis C, brought to an unlikely end by a trial drug program at Cedars Sinai. One minute I'm a fifty-plusser with a terminal disease and a newly pregnant girlfriend, the next I'm gulping some non-FDA approved drug cocktail so toxic it was verboten to touch a pregnant woman. One wrong move and the baby would be born with horns and flippers. Throw in night sweats and you've got yourself a party.)

You could argue that spawning a second child in your fifties represents its own kind of moronic life-affirmation, or you could argue that doing so in the face of impending death and global implosion is an act of such colossal narcissism and folly I should probably be gelded live on the Discovery Channel.

Most disturbing of all, the whole thing leaves me with some kind of—what's the word?—happiness. Sure, I'm embarrassed to still be alive, and just not wanting to throw myself from tall buildings on a daily basis still feels a bit disconcerting. But hey...neurosis was the gift my parents bequeathed me, along with facial moles, unibrow, and a propensity to chafe. And if I have any goal as a damaged Elder-Dad, it's to not pass that depresso-bent along to my offspring.

Sacrifice is (justifiably) a somewhat quaint, if not outright Old Testament-sounding word. But, unless you're a disappearing dad, you've got commitments now. And, unless you're a dick-dad, you're going to put little Seymour or Sally's needs above your own. For me, even after kicking the needle-drugs, life pre-Dadhood was pretty much a non-stop binge cycle of Work, Fuck, Sleep. Self-destruction disguised as creativity. No more, Pops.

The columns you are about to read (or discard, or pass up for an inspirational angel book—my favorite, courtesy of Nick Tosches, being a blessed tome called *God's Mittens*) are here presented as originally typed: each a bloggy snapshot of a particular stop along the newly minted OGD highway. And each as ragged around the edges as the joy-stressed wreck who penned them.

Here's a chestnut: if you're tired of thinking about yourself, have a child. On a good day, guilt and fear trump self-obsession; on a bad one, you can enjoy them all while singing the hits from *Frozen*.

So, go ahead. Pretend it's still your world, Old Guy. No human being under three is ever going to believe it. Which is, unless I'm prematurely demented, exactly how it should be.

#1: The Hur

WAITING FOR A BABY to be born is like sitting in Nagasaki, listening to the hum of planes overhead, and wondering when the little joy bomb is going to be dropped and destroy your life. In a good way. And ours is supposed to drop any minute.

Of course, I've heard the hum before. Been flattened by the thrill and terror of new life delivered from beyond. Only now it's different. For a lot of reasons. Not the least of which is that the first time I staggered into fatherhood I was thirty-five, and strung out, and feeling all the guilt and weirdness over that. And now I'm fifty-eight, and, well...fifty-eight, feeling all the guilt and weirdness over knowing that, no matter how great things are, inevitably I'm going to—Jesus, I can't even say it without cramps—I'm going to be seventy when she's twelve. (The realization, at my age, that seventy is closer than forty, when, in fact, I feel thirty, is a whole other discussion. I mean, who wants to be the creepy old guy on the playground? How do you give horsey rides in a walker?) I don't know why I'm so obsessed. But I can't help it. I harbor this irrational fear that E, the thirty-year-old mom, will have just finished having to change our child's Pampers when she'll begin having to change mine. Two in diapers! Jesus.

I told you, it was irrational. So far I'm footloose and diaper free. But still, some men dream, and some men dread, and I'm a dreader.

Discussing our happy accident, I told E, the thirty-year-old Future Mom, that the night our soon-to-get-here semi-Jew tot was conceived, I imagined I could hear a faint buzzing coming from her vagina. More like a tiny motorized drone: the drone of my sperm chugging along in a Hoveround at the head of a pack, colliding full-on into my sweetheart's egg—not because it was the strongest, or the most worthy, but because it was near-sighted and didn't see the thing. My little Mister Magoo, sputtering accidentally into the miracle of creation.

So now, friends and fans, I'm sitting in Austin—long story, which I'll get to—waiting with the woman of my dreams, while she laments that fact that she's ballooned from a sylph-like 111 to a Hindenburg-esque 150-something. I tell her she's still beautiful, of course, but still… She's been an athlete all her life, and now it's an Olympic event bending to pick up a sock. I used to think that love was damage loving damage—when our pain jibes with the person we're with. Now, I believe, among other things, that it's about "you accept my neurosis and I'll accept yours." Either way, sometimes life can be just too fascinating.

The Austin thing, by the way, is a whole other saga. Which I might as well march out now. This is a column, not literature, so I don't have to worry about seamless transitions. Instead, I can just tell you, in a clunky, intrusive way, I've had hepatitis C for decades, since my stint as a professional needle jockey, back in my days as a dope fiend. (Again, as mentioned, first time around the daddy track I was shooting Mexican tar in the Cedars Sinai OB/GYN men's room in Los Angeles, freaking when the nurse banged on the door and told me the baby was coming, and I had to put on scrubs, not having worn short sleeves in forever, what with the unsightly bleeding tracks and all. But I digress.)

Fast forward to the present. After years of trying every brand of alternative medicine known to man—from coffee enemas and gargling sesame oil, to a vitamin C drip, to injectable ozone therapy, from troughs of wheatgrass, to a trip to the Dominican Republic for illegal stem cell treatment, to daily consumption of enough vitamins and herbal supplements to choke a sea monster, I occasionally felt okay— except for crushing fatigue, night sweats, a roaring, irrational temper (the liver, in Chinese medicine, is the organ of anger), and nonstop brain fog. But I was, on paper, dying just the same. My viral load, as my eighty-year-old, sideburned, ex-surfer hepatologist used to say, "looked like something out of Ray Bradbury. Way up there in the bazillions."

I imagined my liver, not to get too technical, as a dried up old dog turd lodged in my stomach, a hair or two away from cirrhosis. While I lived on in denial, going to the gym, doing Chi Gong, and living my veggie life, it continued to decline. Being a Jewish, vegan Jack LaLanne didn't help.

Long story short, I ended up on this trial drug from Some Major Pharmaceutical

Company—embracing the enemy Big Pharma, after years of fighting for Team Alterna—and sure enough, after one week on a cocktail of AIDS-drug adjacent protease inhibitors and virus killers, my count went from a quarter gazillion down to twenty-three—twenty-three!—and the week after that, be still my heart, down to undetectable.

Mind you, there were side effects, about which I'm not complaining: shortness of breath, weird ingrown hairs that make my chest and legs look like I've taken shrapnel, a constant, crushing spaciness that made every day an adventure in bad acid…etc, etc…(Full disclosure: even though the twelve-week trial's over and I'm still, miracle of miracles, hep free, I have to pop into the hospital every month to see if the evil virus hasn't returned, sending me back down into the shadow of the valley of hep.) But the main side effect, the one that got Future Mom to Austin, is that the stuff was so noxious, so massively mutagenic, that basically just being in the same county as me—well, okay, the same bed—was dangerous, and enough to cause screaming birth defects to any child with the misfortune of being nearby and in utero. Forget sex or intimacy of any kind. It was as though my sperm was now manufactured by Monsanto, and fatal to unborn generations.

How toxic are we talking about? Just touching my finger after that finger had touched a pill, or—god forbid!—coming in contact with my sweat—all of it, any of it, enough to cause the fruit of my loins to emerge—according to the trial administrators—purple with wheels. Hence, for the months I was on the trial, she went to be with her people in Austin, while I, back in poison bachelorville, remained in Los Angeles.

#2: The Texa Jew l

s
Panel
WEEK 39, DAY 2

FOR REASONS I EXPLAINED last time around, we are having our little she-creature in Austin, which has a reputation as the hipster heart of Texas. But whatever enlightenment has pooled in this wet spot in the center of the Lone Star State, it did not seem to spill over into the Perinatal Clinic, to which our OB/GYN has dispatched us, in order to screen for every infant malady known to man. All well and good, until, filling out a form by the frosted glass window, the beehived lovely in charge of our application raised her eyes and asked, in a tone somewhere between blasé and pre-chunk blowing, "So, like, are Jews Caucasians?"

I just looked at her. "What?"

This time, another nurse-slash-receptionist type stuck her head out, doing little to hide her distaste, and barked in a voice loud enough to rouse the *New Mommy* magazine readers in the far corner of the waiting room, "Sir, we have to do a *Jew Panel*."

"Excuse me?"

For one *brief* second I thought I saw the ghost of Mengele waft over the counter. He used to measure noses with calipers, to sniff out latent Semites.

"Jew Panel," she repeated. "We don't get a lot of your people around here. We need to check for Tay-Sachs and cystic fibrosis."

Turning away, I felt a dozen sets of Texan eyes upon me as I rolled back to take my seat beside my blue-eyed, blonde-haired, Viking-ette girlfriend. She saw the look on my face. "Jesus, baby, what's wrong?"

"Nothing's wrong," I lied. "I just hope we make it back to the car without getting rounded up and sent to some Panhandle Auschwitz. Most places, they at least try to pretend they don't hate you.

"They don't hate you. It's Texas," she said sounding like the guy who tells Jack Nicholson, "Come on, Jake, it's Chinatown," at the end of the Polanski movie. Right after John Huston shoots Faye Dunaway and scoops up her wailing, product-of-incest daughter.

Happily, all tests proved negative, but even without that soupcon of regional bigotry, there's a certain weirdness to every aspect of childbearing. Especially now, when Tiny Screamer could be popping out any second. Nine times a day, my girlfriend and Future Mom asks me to reach over and feel the baby kicking. (And, forgive me, I'm not going to say Baby Mama; it reminds of pinstriped, barely post-pube Hollywood agents who greet each other with "Whassup, dawg?" and "Yo, homey!" like they're straight out of Compton, instead of straight off of Wilshire Boulevard, in Beverly Hills. And I say this with love.)

"Look it's her little foot," my girlfriend will coo. And, no doubt it is. (I mean, it couldn't be a shiv, could it?) But to me the whole deal still feels like touching a weasel trapped in a water balloon.

Truth be told, the whole concept of carrying a baby feels like transporting a body in a trunk. As though, at the end of term, instead of the obstetrician in scrubs, Joe Pesci and De Niro will be waiting with shovels and hacksaws. I'm not proud of this, but every time

I put my fingertips to the roving baby bulges, I half expect hands to come bursting out, like the ones that Catherine Deneuve hallucinated exploding out of the walls in *Repulsion.*

Mind you, I couldn't be happier about looming fatherdom. It's not the bundle of joy that's the issue here. It's all the stuff leading up to it. For one thing, when you're going to have a baby, other babies know. I'm convinced. You can see it in their eyes. The way they glare you at you out of their Peanut Shell adjustable baby slings, as if to say, *One of us is on the way. Be ready, Sucker!* It's the opposite of cuddly. Cross paths with a toddler in an airport, a deli, wherever, and you can almost hear them, mocking. *Better man up, Shlomo, cause a lovable four-limbed poop-grenade is about to blow up your life.* Whoever you are, unless you're at the Mitt Romney car elevator, full-time night nurse, live-in nanny, and diapers-woven-from-hundred-dollar-bills end of the spectrum, you're going to be reduced—or nominated—to Wiper in Chief.

But even that's fine. I had no problem manning the Pampers with my first child, still the proverbial apple of my eye. Mind you, now she's twenty-three, meaning, for some time now, that I've been free to obsess about myself and not worry my hoary little head about meeting her every need. Even now there is no certainty— the world being what it is—that something heinous might not happen to her, but chances are this would not involve falling out of a crib and crushing her soft spot, or eating glass off the floor. Without a doubt, at twenty-three, I might have done some glass-eating. But thank my lucky stars, my First Daughter, thus far, has shown no such inclinations. She's talented, smart, beautiful, and clearly the product of her mother's genes. (Otherwise she'd be waxing a unibrow.)

No, wait—I have to stop! Contractions coming faster and faster! In fact, we were halfway to the hospital, on the line to the doctor, who announced that it was probably just a Braxton-Hicks contraction. What are Braxton-Hicks? They're the Milli Vanilli of imminent childbirth indicators, faux-squeezers that mimic actual contractions, by way—some theorize—of giving the soon-to-be mom a taste of the real thing. "Practice contractions," as the doctor explained it. Of course, Braxton-Hicks sounds like a British art band from the seventies. The Fripp & Eno era. But they're an actual medical occurrence. Source of many a false alarm. And so, we turn around. And head back to the launching pad.

#3:
Insan
in the
Meml

e

orane

S O, WE'RE BACK IN the OB/GYN waiting room. Our baby still hasn't come. The suspense, as they say, is killing me. The walls are hung with photos of other peoples' babies—half in sunglasses, a practice, for some reason, that creeps me out even more than Ray-Bans on dogs. Though, somehow, shades look okay on cats. Life's a mystery.

Weirdly, an attractive, yet massively-lipsticked, chinless woman facing us flashes a semi-beaver. Pink pencil skirt crawling up her parted thighs to reveal Hot Mama panties. This isn't a judgment of some kind. The panties literally say "Hot Mama" across the crotch, in red on white, over the faux-imprint of a red-lipped kiss. Impossible to look at, impossible not to. E, noticing me noticing, dismisses the display with a shrug. "Cry for help."

We sit another moment. Leafing through an old issue of *New Mom*—the cover sports a catchy headline, *"SAY GOODBYE TO YOUR HORRI-BELLY!"*—before she blows blonde hair out of her face, drops the mag, and sighs. "I'm always uncomfortable coming here. It's like I know when I walk in that examining room I'm going to be fisted. But not in a good way."

Not much I can say to that.

Minutes later, we're ushered in to the exam room. Minutes after that, E's back in the stirrups, and the blue-uniformed nurse, who could be a twelve-year-old Nina Simone, gels up the heartbeat monitor, which looks like a karaoke mike, and plants it on her mega-watermelon belly. Instantly, a sound like horror movie wraiths dragging rusty chains across the floor fills the room. When this bit of Wes Craven entertainment is over, young Nina announces the heart rate—a stellar 143—and tells us the doctor would be here in a sec.

Like clockwork, a half hour later, the doctor whisks in, chipper as Ruth Gordon in *Rosemary's Baby,* and smiles big. "Okay. What we're going to do today is strip the membrane." Explaining as she slides her fingers into the latex sado-glove, she bids E to lean back and slides her arm in up to the elbow. My girlfriend begins to writhe on the table. I jump out of the chair, to the head of the examination table. E grabs my hand and squeezes as the doctor narrates.

"Okay, what I'm doing is placing my fingers in the opening of the cervix…Mmmmph…Trying to—Ooof!—gently separate the amniotic sac from the uterus."

When I can suppress my gorge long enough to form words, I squeak, "What, um, does this do exactly?"

"Well, after around the fortieth week, membrane stripping stimulates the release of prostaglandin."

My head is spinning so fast, seeing my girlfriend endure medieval torment, that what I hear is "pasta glands," which clearly can't be right. "I'm sorry," I manage, "can you, um—"

"Prostaglandin. It's the hormone that softens the cervix to prepare it for labor."

By now, E has squeezed my fingers to total numbness.

"There's going to be some pain, and a bit of bleeding," the doctor goes on, withdrawing her hand and ripping off the blood-tamped glove with a flourish. "But, if all goes well, we should see you go into labor within forty-eight hours. So, how do you feel?"

"Like I've been raped by a potato peeler."

Big chuckle from doctor. "I'm on call Tuesday. Call me before then if you have any problems."

Helping my sore, but admirably uncomplaining, girlfriend off the table, I wait while she gets dressed, recalling a spectacularly ludicrous argument we had months ago, on a visit to our first obstetrician in Los Angeles. This was at the dawn of pregnancy. We'd tracked down an OB/GYN over the hill, in Burbank, who said he preferred it if we called him "Dr. Tug." Tug turned out to be a burly, marathon-running seventy-one-year-old who played Motown in his examination room and kept his sleeves rolled-up to the shoulders, showing off his guns. This lent him a strange, unseemly resemblance to an obstetric Mr. Clean.

During the first exam, with me in the room, Tug got my girlfriend up in the stirrups, then asked, over a rumbling, bass-heavy Barry White, what she did for a living. E filled him in, explaining that she was an exercise rider, working, most recently, at Santa Anita, powering world-class thoroughbreds full speed around the track every morning before the races. In truth, she'd been banging around the country, working on the back side of racetracks since she left home at fourteen, giving her a history even more dangerous and crazy than my own, which is one of the things that attracted me to her. If I thought junkiedom was hard-core—the world she ran in was a whole other level. E was addicted to speed, but not the narcotic kind. Her fix was the kind that put you in danger of a broken neck, or shattered skull, or brutal violent death on a daily basis. How could you not love a woman that bad-ass? But Doctor Tug had a different take.

"You ride horses," he chuckled. "That explains those beautiful legs."

Admittedly, she does have amazing legs. But really, do you want to hear your obstetrician talking about them? If this weren't bad enough, a minute later, while he was all up inside her, the old beefcake got—I will swear this to my grave—a dreamy smile on his face. As soon as I saw this, I was ready to snap. But a second later, while still probing—"Looks good in there!"—he exchanged a little smile with E herself. Again, I managed to hold my mud. But back in the car, I'm not going to lie, I had to bring it up.

"So," I said, "you like this guy?"

"He's all right. The important thing is, everything seems to be okay."

"Of course," I agree, regretting what I'm about to say even before I say it, "but what I'm talking about is, you seemed to, I don't know, enjoy the examination."

"Come again?"

"I don't know," I babble on, feeling myself lurch deeper into idiocy with every syllable. I'm not the jealous type, but this is just too much. I turn the key in my old Caddy's ignition and continue. "I'm just saying, when he was inside you…it's kind of fucked up, but he looked like… he looked like he was *enjoying* himself. You had this smile on your face, you know, the one you sometimes get when…anyway, he'd already made that creepy remark about your legs, so I thought maybe—"

"You thought what?"

By now I know I've crossed the line. This has all the makings of an epic car fight. But instead of yelling, E— to her eternal credit— just turns to me as we peel out of the lot, and laughs in my face.

"Are you *insane?* First of all, that's a completely bizarre thing to even think. Second of all, the man is gay. Didn't you see all those pictures of him and his partner? While you were in the bathroom he told me he and Ted were happily married."

"Really?" I hear myself sputter. "Did his hand feel gay when it was inside you?"

My eyes stay on the road as we nose onto the Hollywood Freeway.

"Holy shit! You're jealous of a gynecologist?"

"Of course not," I lie, and have to swerve to miss a fuel truck, barely managing to spare the three of us—Future Mom, future baby, and currently babbling dad—a fiery, horrific death.

By the time we make it back to my place, we're both laughing about it. Sort of. But later, talking to a few fathers of my acquaintance, all confessed to some version of what my friend Willie, a guitar player, calls Gyno Up My Wife Syndrome, which usually manifests the first time a man sees another man sliding his hand up the woman he loves. Often—or so it seems—wearing a dreamy, distracted smile on his face. Or worse, talking about "how wonderful" everything feels in there.

This is not something I'm proud of. But, hey, fatherhood is a journey of discovery. And OG Dads—having to deal with receptionists who mistake them for the patient's father, not to mention nonstop sweat-soaked three a.m. meditations on their own mortality—may just get a little more winded going uphill...

Ah, memories. Back in real time, here in Austin, I help the now-racked-with-pain E up into the taint-colored Honda Crossover I've purchased to handle baby duties. And yes, possibly more traumatic than the fact that I'm going to be a father again in my fifties is the fact that I'm now driving the four-wheeled equivalent of cotton Dockers in Texas. But that's a different discussion for a different time. This, after all, is not about me.

#4: Stir Crazy.

JESUS, THIS FUCKING WAITING! It's like, if I were paranoid, I would actually be wondering if this baby-to-be kind of hates us. Or, more accurately, hates *me*. What's going on there in Wombville? Has she heard me fart? Why is she shunning our invitation? Last to leave the party in mommy-gut...

Being the type who never acknowledges stress or emotion, and instead drives blithely into phone poles while chewing his tongue, I have, during this (massively long) wait for our overdue daughter, developed a festive rash on my face. Think pepper spray victim, or ringworm, but more garish. It's the kind of look that makes strangers back away slowly at the supermarket, groping for Purell.

What happened, see, during our last visit to the baby doctor, was that she mentioned, casually, that there was a mini-outbreak of leprosy in Austin. Well, actually, more of a minor plague…okay, one lonely case. But still. Less than three hours later, I began to break out in fire engine-red blotches, lumps, and pustules across my forehead. And let's not even talk about the itch (I once had a pal in first grade who wiped his ass with poison oak in the woods. I imagine now my face feels like his sphincter felt). Seriously, I am so itchy, I stand in front of the mirror with a cheese grater, thinking, *Should I?*

Anyway, that night, between painful contractions, false alarms, and bloody panty-liner panic (a result of the membrane stripping, see chapter three), my girlfriend offers a bit of old racetrack wisdom, suggesting the best thing for an out-of-control rash was—what else?—a nice hot oatmeal bath. All well and good, except that, not being a look-at-the-label type, E grabbed the organic oats off the shelf, then dumped them around me in, as Mitt Romney would say, severely hot water.

So, voila! In three minutes, like some lost episode of the Lucy show, there I am, sitting in a batch of beautifully congealed, ready-to-eat oatmeal.

"Well," said E, blessed with an unimpeachable deadpan, "should we add raisins or just dump you in the disposal?"

All of which I mention, not to hammer home the fact that life, on occasion, imitates sitcom, but to demonstrate the depths to which two humans, unable to really go anywhere or do anything, having been told that childbirth is imminent, will descend. I mean, where *do* you want to be when your water breaks? The circus? An Olive Garden? Watching a Vin Diesel movie?

No, we're playing it safe. Staying at home, in a palatial three-micro-roomed rental in Hyde Park, Austin, scoping MSNBC, trying to write, snacking out on elaborate avocado, walnut, and mystery toast concoctions, reading or walking our basenji all day. (Writers, you know, have a little extra free time.) But, speaking of basenji, I heartily recommend this breed for anyone who wants a dog but does not, you know, want a *dog*-dog. They don't bark, they sleep like cats, they tend to have the same face as the late-inning, alcoholic Judy Garland—and, best of all, you can wear them around your neck, like their original owners, Gambian antelope hunters, were wont to do in ancient times. How do I know this? Google, of course. You tend to do a lot of Googling when you're cooped up waiting for your fucking baby to be born. (Wait—did I just write "fucking baby?" Jesus! Strike that from the record! I already love that little scoop of ice cream more than life and living. I just wish Satan would move things along.)

Speaking of Google, did you know that Benjamin Franklin invented tampons? Stick around!

After an afternoon spent alternately studying her belly-globe—"Hey, come here, feel how hard this is!"—finishing Joshua Mohr's insanely great novel *Termite Parade*, absorbing coverage of Obama's gay marriage announcement, E Googled Crystal Ball, her fave political commentator, and found a photo of her mouthing a dildo at a Christmas party, thereby cementing her girl-crush. "I love her," she says, showing me the picture. "She's brilliant as shit, and she knows how to have a good time."

I have to agree. "Show me Wolf Blitzer fondling a sex toy, and maybe that bearded minge would be halfway watchable."

And so it goes. The proverbial elephant in the room is the unborn newborn herself. But we talk around it, puttering like addled rest home residents, already sleep-deprived, not from some wailing crumb-cruncher, but from the weird festering pressure of knowing what's in the mail. E is terrified—as who wouldn't be?—of the pain to come, and, simultaneously, terrified the pain won't *ever* come. What will come, what keeps coming, are drops of panty-staining blood, mysterious rib anguish, palpitations, shuddering fetal kidney-kicks, and so on. "Oh Jesus...*fuck!*" she'll shriek. "It feels like someone is wrenching my uterus out with a clawhammer."

Now it's evening. E's belly is a roiling maw of agony, her feet swollen as a marathon dancer as she and I go about the business of repacking the "hospital bag" the doctor advised us to pack, making sure we know where the car keys are—I can't swear it's not early senility on my part, but they keep surfacing in the freezer—and, last but not least, helping haul her newly ample ass off the couch, to look for her baby papers. These, while too complicated to describe, are nothing compared to the Cord Blood pack. We've signed on to save the umbilical cord blood, for stem cell purposes— who knows when you'll need a batch?—but the red tape involved alone is enough to incline one to brain surgery, preferably lobotomy. (January Jones, apparently, freeze-dried her placenta and munches it like corn chips, but we're still on the fence about placenta snacks.)

In any event, here we are, in a private cocoon of expectation, literally waiting for agony, for ecstasy, for whatever combo platter of lifelong joy, obligation, pressure, weirdness, fun, and crushing debt is to come. The greatest moment of my life—and excuse me if I'm all dewy-eyed, but cynics, as Voltaire once said (or was it Cher?), are just failed romantics—the greatest moment of my life was feeling my now-grown daughter's tiny form on my chest, when she herself was newly hatched. And the prospect of going through it again, of getting the opportunity, what can I say, to do it on the natch, is just too much. The first time, thanks for asking, there was some heroin involved. And now, well now, call me a wild man, it's more about 4:00 a.m. guacamole and 2:00 p.m. naps. But a man's got to do what a man's got to do.

But who am I kidding? If that fucking baby doesn't get here soon, I'm going to need an epidural myself.

#5:
The Anal
Cauliflow
Other Wo
the Pregn

r, and
ders of
nt World

S O IT'S THE MIDDLE of the night and I hear screaming. It's the baby, trapped in E's watermelon belly, and she's not happy. Ear pressed to this taut flesh-bubble, I can't tell if the little squib's yelping "Let me out" or "Who fucking stuck me in here?"

I wake up gnawing my own fist and stagger to the window, gasping for air in the muggy mosquito farm that is Austin in springtime... "It's just a dream," E mumbles. "Right, right," I say, rubbing my skin. But my relief is short-lived. Once my brain defogs, I instantly flash to our earlier OB/GYN visit, where once again, we bought our popcorn and plunked down in front of the ultrasound monitor.

This time, our camera-shy little girl decided to block the camera like Madonna dodging the paparazzi, covering her face with her elbow. Only according to the doctor, she wasn't being coy—she was sucking her arm. "She's…what?"

"Sucking her arm. Lots of babies do it. It's sort of like practice-suckling. Though I have to warn you, she might show up with a hickey."

E raised her head on the table, dizzy from doctor-probing. "Wh-what? A hickey?"

"On her arm, obviously," the doctor chuckled. "It may take a while to break her of the habit."

Naturally, I bite my lip. If I don't I'm going to blurt out my paranoid fantasy. "What the fuck, is she going to show up with a *stump?*"

I know, I know. I'm not proud. It's just—how to explain?—there's a particular species of paranoia particular to looming childbirth. And thanks to the wonders of our friend the internet—half party-sewer, half enlightenment-engine—it's impossible not to feed it. Add to this the specifically bizarro circumstances of our current situation, waiting for the penny to drop—no, waiting for it to drop the rest of the way—advised by medical professionals to stay close, not do much, lay low… Well, Christ, how *not* to go online? Or—if you happen to be wired like my high-IQ, hard-core, life-experience girlfriend—how not to instantly start trolling through worst-case scenario pregnancy videos?

I'll skip the opening act. But let me just say, without embellishment, that the Anal Cauliflower has to take the Oscar for all-time "worst shit that can happen short of death or life-threatening problems" video. What am I talking about? Well, deep in the bowels of cyberspace, there is a mother who felt compelled to go before a camera and share her epic pregnancy-induced sphincter and skin-tag trauma. There, I said it.

What happened, see, is that—for lack of a more tactful description—this mommy's anus exploded into a festival of skin-tags. I am not talking about a few. We all have a few. I'm talking hundreds. Maybe thousands. On-screen, all I can tell you, is that something resembling a cauliflower protruded out of her nether-cheeks, rendering (according to her own testimony) basic bodily functions a daily horror, driving her husband out of the room when she undressed for bed, and last, but hardly least, making the act of childbirth what can only be described as a colossally painful, unspeakably shameful hell-fest.

(On a personal note, it is a beloved family story how my own mother, god bless her, made no secret of how much she resented me for giving her hemorrhoids when she squeegeed my tiny, guilt-ridden bottom into the world, half a century ago. Family!)

Which takes us back to the Anal Cauliflower. Poor E, projecting all her (understandable) dread of the unknown on this unlikely malady, makes me promise I'll hang in with her, even if she sprouts some heinous, between-the-cheeks skin-tag bouquet of her own.

"Of course!" I say. "But it's not going to happen. I promise. If it does, I'll handle it."

I almost say, *We'll sell tickets!* But, as I've discovered, borderline-dickish humor doesn't really work with a pregnant woman. At least, not this pregnant woman. (And, really, when does it ever pay to be a borderline dick? Unless you're Mitt Romney?) Instead, what I say is, "Why don't we head out to Walgreens, lay in some liquid nitrogen and scissors, just in case?"

"Talk about a dream date," she snaps, and I know things are back on keel.

Okay, then. Having cleared the Anal Cauliflower hurdle, made it through the whole baby-sucking-her-arm syndrome, and survived my stroll down maternal hemorrhoid memory lane, E and I are finally free to kick back and do what we now do best—stress about when the fuck the little object of our affection is going to get off the dime and hightail it down the birth canal.

"I swear, I don't think she's ever coming," E says, shrinking into the couch with her basenji, Alvin, sprawled lewdly on her lap, as he is wont to sprawl, legs up and splayed in some X-rated opposition to the elegant Asta of *Thin Man* fame. Alvin's as louche as Asta was cute. But great company when you're going out of your skull from late term pregnancy, or, in my case, incipient, itchy leprosy. (I know leprosy doesn't itch—your shit just falls off.) But something in this bug-drippy Austin humidity does not agree with me, and for days now my face looks like something dermatology students would sneak pictures of and pass around at parties.

Still, reaching over and stroking the barkless dog's spotted belly, I try to rise above, and think of something reassuring to say.

"Listen," I begin, trying in my ham-fisted way to put a chipper spin on the situation. "Horrible analogy, okay, but it reminds me of when I was freshly relapsed, out of rehab, and living with a lady mechanic in Phoenix."

"A lady mechanic? Really?"

"No longer with us," I say, only a little defensively. "Or maybe she is. I don't know. The point is, I used to spend every day waiting for the FedEx guy to arrive with the heroin I had mailed in from LA. After a month, I'd self-Pavloved to the point where I could make out the axle squeak of the FedEx van from five blocks away. I mean, I'd be jonesing, I'd be dying—my dealer only got it together to mail shit once every few days—but suddenly, when I'd pretty much given up hope, when I was, like, totally bottomed out—*ske-REEEEEE*—here comes FedEx!"

"So what you're saying is…?"

Jesus, what *am* I saying? "Well," I faloomph, "I guess…what I'm saying is, you know… Oh, fuck it, I don't know what I'm saying, let's just fucking roll with it, okay? You're nine months pregnant, the baby's not going to sneak off under cover of darkness, you're seeing the doctor every few days, and there's really no way out but the way she came in…"

"So?"

"So let's see what's on TV. I think Colbert's on."

"Good idea."

And then—cue kettle drums—she feels something big.

#6:
Dope-A

-Mom

WEEK 39, DAY 6

HERE WE ARE, BACK in the doctor's office. Our home away from home. We've come, yet again, to try and see why our unborn party ball has yet to start its descent into humanity. (When we last left off, we thought Apocalypse was Now. But it turned out to be more teaser pain.) Post-membrane stripping, the last four days, for E, have been divided between dripping blood between her legs and stomach-clutching, seemingly random contractions. Ergo, she is more than ready to go Enola Gay and drop the big one.

"At this point," my weary perma-cramped girlfriend tells the doctor, "this baby doesn't need to be born—she needs to be evicted."

The doctor, rooting in E's uterus like she's lost her wallet, just smiles distractedly.

E sighs, talking to the ceiling. "This baby. It's like—*ouch, easy!*—it's like she's one of those old Manhattan ladies who won't leave her apartment, even though the wrecking ball's coming. She's in there with her canary, twelve cats, and a doily collection. And she's not going anywhere."

"Well," the doctor says, pulling off her gloves, "you've got a nice soft cervix. Of course it's only two-and-a-half centimeters. So it could be a while."

The due date's come and gone. (Which, between us, was fine with me, since she was supposed to be born on Mother's Day, and the idea of having to conflate this child's birthday with sullen brunching families for the next twenty years (assuming I'm around for a few of them) is not something I'd regret foregoing. All that faux love and guilt floating around might do something to a girl's self-esteem. Then again, my own mother, god bless her, liked to spend family vacations throwing up on national monuments—*Oh look, the Liberty Bell! BLEECCCCCH!*—and I turned out almost fine.

"How long can this go on?" E asks, keeping the fear I know she harbors out of her voice.

She's one of those raised-by-wolves types who doesn't parade her emotions at the drop of a bowler. But I know, because she's told me, she harbors fear of ending up as some News of the Weird item about the mom who carried her child so long it was born a pre-pube.

And so, the decision is made to induce. To kick-start birth. For a few reasons. Mostly, E's in staggering pain. But also, naturally, the doctor, a rare and tiny combination of competent and bubbly, whom E adores, is going to a medical convention in Cancun, and will be leaving in two days. By the time she comes back with a tan and an International House of Obstetrics gift bag, E could be cruising into week forty-two. That, or she will go into labor, and will have to be attended to by one of Dr. Tiny's partners, who, while doubtless great guys, all have the jocky, golden boy swagger of Texas high school quarterbacks. The kind of dils who would have grabbed me in the gym locker, hung me upside down, and tied macaroons to my penis when I was young and Jewy. Which is a whole different story.

"Come in tomorrow morning," the doctor says—after stripping E's membrane again. (By now, I imagine, the thing must look like pastrami.) "I'll inject you with Pitocin. This kicks in the oxytocin."

Naturally I perk up. "OxyContin? The body produces that?" Funny thing about being clean for a while—you can be off the hard stuff for decades, and, at mention of a freebie, your brain just kicks right back to junky-think. As in—*Wait, women produce hillbilly heroin when they have babies? Why can't I get pregnant?*

"Not OxyContin, oxytocin," the doctor quickly corrects me. "It's a naturally occurring hormone, produced in the brain and released into the bloodstream during labor. It creates feelings of contentment. Reduces anxiety, gives you a feeling of security and calm. It's kind of blissful, actually. When you feel it, your uterus contracts."

"Is it dangerous?" E asks, though not in a way that suggests danger is a *bad* thing. I can see her fighting off fresh torment from the re-membrane rip. People who risk flying off of 2,000-pound animals for a living tend not to make a thing of their own suffering. (Unlike say, my family, who all subscribed to Mel Brooks' dictum: "Tragedy is I get a hangnail, comedy is you slip on a banana peel and die.")

Our little doctor exudes reassurance. "Sometimes inducing does increase the risk of a caesarian. Which—aside from the fact that it's, you know, *surgery*—means the baby won't get all that good, immune-boosting flora and fauna when it passes through the birth canal vaginally."

"Flora and fauna. That sounds so rainforesty."

"I know," I say, "I get this image of a toddler being dragged on a bobsled through the Amazon."

"In a way," the doctor says. "Babies are born with a sterile digestive track. They need this introduction of bacteria and such for digestion, and detoxing heavy metals. And the best way to get it is through their mouth, nose, and ears when they're coming out of mom."

Somehow, I wonder if this means cunnilingus is a great way to avoid colds. But it seems wrong to ask. E looks at me and shrugs, "Let's hope for vaginal." Then she turns back to the doctor. "What about the oxy-stuff? What are the risks?"

The question rates a hearty doctor-chuckle. "Oxytocin? Well, some people call it The Love Hormone. I suppose there is a danger you'll want to kiss the UPS man or something. It's also released during the stimulation of a woman's nipples, to help New Moms bond with baby."

I want to know why this shit isn't bottled and sold on the street, but, again, this is probably not the moment to ask. For now, it's time to help E haul her ever-expanding self off the table, wait while she gets dressed, then head back to the little waiting room we call home and hang out till tomorrow morning, when we're supposed to hit the hospital bright and early, at 6:00 a.m., and get the show on the road.

•　　　•　　　•

ONLY IT DOESN'T WORK out that way. By that afternoon, E is walking around gasping and clutching her stomach. Finally it gets so bad that *I* break water. It happens when I'm writing on the bed and she staggers out of the bathroom, doubles over, and screams, which startles me so much I break the glass of water I'm holding in my hands, soaking my Mac keyboard. At which point, after I wipe it off, the cursor begins to dance crazily around the screen, skittering sideways and up and down, opening and closing files at will. I break computers the way Sinatra broke heads.

But no time to think about that now. E is on the floor, curled up in pain. "Don't think this is working," she says, with typical hard-ass blonde understatement.

I see the small pool of blood between her legs and that's it. "Fuck this. I'm calling the doctor... We're going in."

• • •

A HALF-HOUR LATER, WE'RE at the hospital, walking into the most soulless, depressing four walls I've stepped into since the time I was flown in on the wrong day for a book tour and spent an entire twenty-four hours hunkered in a Milwaukee Days Inn. Except that, unlike my Milwaukee shame motel, this one has a handy medi-nook. In one corner is a table with a glass case on top, stocked with mask, stethoscope, powder blue surgical cap, and matching knit baby beanie. It looks like a museum display—or something you break in case of emergency, like a fireman's axe in the stairwell of a Forties office building.

E changes into an okra-colored hospital gown while the first of what will be a parade of nurses, administrators, anesthesiologists, and doctors paddles in with a stack of papers.

"First off," says Nurse Number One, a spritely, young, albino-adjacent Texan by the name of Tee-Tee, "we gotta ask y'all some questions."

Mind you, at this point, E has gone so agony-white herself that translucent is a step up. But, as Tee-Tee explains "I'm sorry, Pregnant Lady, but we can't do a thing till I get in these forms."

(She actually says this, "Pregnant Lady," sounding like Will Farrell doing George W, in blonde wig and blue nurse's uniform.)

And then it begins. "Social Security?... Birthday?... Age?... Home Phone?... Height... Weight before pregnancy?... Weight now?... College?... Work?... Religious preference?... Allergies?... Special diet?...Skin infection?... Surgery?... Antibiotics?... Rehabs?... HIV?"

By now it's pouring outside. Thunder, lighting. Pitch black. Branches thrashing against the window. E answers through clenched teeth, like some Civil War wounded, about to have a limb hacked off by a barber holding a glass of whiskey. Half of me wonders what happens if she says, "Yes, as a matter of fact, I *am* a drug-addicted scabies victim with no education, AIDS, an allergy to soap, and a diet of ham hocks?" What are they going to do then? Throw her out? (This being America, probably.)

The session ends with a glass-rattling thunderclap, followed by the appearance of a woman of size named Shareesa who sweeps in wheeling a drug table on wheels, not a moment too soon.

"I think Miss E's had enough for now," she snaps, dismissing the pigment-free L'il Inquisitor, rolling right over, and taking my girlfriend's head in her hands. "Okay, honey, one to ten, how much pain would you say you're in?"

"I don't know…six?"

"Oh, look at you," says Shareesa, "you a hard case, huh? Would you like some relief, sweetie? We have something called Stadol we usually give at this stage."

"Stay-doll?" I hear myself repeat. What six-figure pharma-genius consultant came up with that name? "Stay doll" for a drug that keeps women drugged up enough to lie there and not run screaming into the night while undergoing the hell-party necessary to bring life into the world. Why not go all the way and call it *Dope-A-Mom*? *Or just Mommy-Junk*?

"It's a synthetic opioid," Shareesa informs us. "What we do, we give you the painkiller, along with something called Phenergan for the nausea."

"You sure it's okay? I don't want the baby to come out addicted to drugs."

"The way it looks, you won't be delivering for a while. They'll be out of your system by then."

By now, it's obvious that E's in scalding torment. Just watching her talk makes me want to eat my arms. "For Christ's sake," I tell her, "take the fucking drugs. If the baby comes out and steals your wallet, I take full responsibility."

If nothing else, nurse and patient bond over their complete lack of amusement at my remark. And on we go.

While she loads the syringe, Shareesa makes delivery room small talk. "Now the strangest baby names I ever heard? That would be Orangejello and Lemonjello. What I hear, the mama named 'em that cause these were her two favorite Jell-Os. You see it all up in here, honey."

Another up periscope uterine moment, after which, while Shareesa takes some vitals and puts them in the computer, she casually lays out the game plan. "Now, sweetie, we're at an important point in your labor process. Projecting five to ten hours till showtime. Once that Tiny Screamer is out, you all might not get another chance to sleep for more than two hours at a time for the next year. At least. You should take advantage of this lull, and get some rest. Daddy, I already ordered y'all a rollaway."

As if in cue, an orderly comes in pushing a foldout cot, blankets, and sheets. What our incarcerated friends might refer to as a rollup. Except, this is a different kind of holding cell. And, in my case, instead of heading off to Quentin, I'm catching the chain to Old Guy Dad Supermax.

While I set up, E raises her head from her bed of pain, smiles crookedly. "Baby," she croaks, her voice a register or nine lower than normal. "I am fucked up!" *

After Shareesa paddles out, we try to take her advice. Chill out, watch a little TV, and doze. (Naturally, I'd meant to bring an iPod, with speakers, and it's still sitting on a coffee table with my five spirulina bars.) For some reason every time we stop dozing there's nothing on the tube but no!no! hair removal ads. Is it an infomericial? A conspiracy? An alien plot? "Try no!no!" screams the idiot TV voice. "Thirty days risk free! Remove your hair on the go!" At which point, unless I'm hallucinating, the TV shows some grinning douchebag driving a convertible while removing hair from his pecs. E and I both nod off. But whenever we look up, there's no!no!-douche beaming from the screen, shaving his busy exec pecs on the go.

Twenty minutes—or two hours—later, my eyes open on another nurse, this one a Latina named Luz with weirdly adorable giant ears, come to measure E's cervix again. As she works between my girlfriend's legs, she tells us she's supposed to move this weekend, but her *puta* fiancé left all her furniture out in the rain. (Did I mention it's pouring out? I did, right? It's been a long night.) "From two centimeters to four take forever," Nurse Luz explains, with a lilting straight-outa-Juarez accent. But from four to ten—ten, basically, being Bouncing Babyhead Circumference—things move about a centimeter an hour

One thing we have going for us, apparently, is barometric pressure. It's storming like fuck out there. And a big pressure drop supposedly helps kick in the birth process…which is exactly what it does. Eventually.

At some point—indulge me here—things just begin to swirl. It's like, E got the drugs, but I got disembodied. Nurse after nurse comes in, each uniformly kind, and each larger than the one before. (What do they feed them in this hospital?) I blink awake in time to hear another RN, wheeling another portable computer monitor combo, lean over the fitfully sleeping E, and announce, "Okay, darlin', cold gel alert. I've got stubby old fingers, so hang on. Now lean back and spread your legs like a fried chicken."

On comes the light and, not for the last time that night, I cast around for somewhere to aim my eyes while a medical professional hovers over E's crotch, armed with everything but a miner's hat.

"Um-hmm, um-hmm…Very nice. Four centimeters," the nurse goes on. "Very, very nice."

Then, out of nowhere, E screams, nearly jerks off the table, and the nurse presses a buzzer. "We're gonna get you something else to help you relax."

"Not the Stadol," E pleads, "I hate that shit."

"Oh don't worry, hon, we'll get you something better than that. It's still gonna be a while till showtime."

Fast forward another hour or three, and E is out cold, propped up on the hospital bed, attached to a fetal monitor, blasting sounds from the womb, while I lie on my back on the plasti-wrapped mattress, eying the flailing branches lit by lightning outside... The unborn child's heartbeat thrums in the dark like some kind of faroff, roiling army, forever approaching. It's straight out of Poe, *The Telltale Heart.* Except it's not the heart of a dead man I can hear, it's the heart of a not-yet-living child. This disembodied thump-thump, thump-thump, thump-thump.

Louder. Closer. Stronger.

When I close my eyes, it's almost like the beating is inside my own chest.

#7:
A
Stahl
is Bo

rn

SPOILER ALERT: I'M WRITING this with a half-day-old, six-pound, nine-ounce newborn and Patton Oswalt look-alike Baby N curled in my left arm, typing one-handed with a precariously balanced MacBook on my crotch (the radiation thus insuring she'll have no brothers or sisters) breathing betadine fumes and wondering whether the roar blasting through my heart is love, sleeplessness, or backed-up hospital waffles.

Don't let the idyllic lead full you. The night behind us has been so *Game of Thrones*-y that even now the blood squishes underfoot, the floor is littered with cast-off scarlet rags, stained plastic gloves. And the sound of wailing is never far off or faraway. In fact, let's rewind, since the screaming's still in my ears.

About twenty hours and a few spinning worlds ago, in a delivery room down the hall from where I'm writing this, E writhed at the center of a hive of medical pros, screaming as though cleaved down the middle. Which eventually she was. (Twenty-five stitches—thanks for asking!) The reason we're still here—fun fact—is that Texas requires newborns to spend two days in the hospital before they're released. They also execute a boatload of grown-ups every year, so it evens out.

Anyway, hours before the Main Event, after being jarred from a half-sleep—where I was dreaming, weirdly, of Karl Rove in bonnet and Mampers—I lay for a minute, meditating on the event at hand. The birth of a child. There are probably a thousand profound things to say. Observations on mortality, the cycle of life, birth, death… The ghosts of the Holocaust swirling over the hospital, abuzz at the prospect of a Juden merged with a woman who might have been on the cover of *Master Race Monthly.* (Hot Shiksa action!) But I'm not that deep. What I'm thinking about is the way this rollaway mattress bites into my knee, as I try to steal a last thirty-nine winks before the curtains part.

When E's contractions reach epic proportion, and Stadol can no longer stay her, Shareesa, the nurse we'd met what seemed like years ago—actually twelve hours earlier, at the end of her shift—powers in, remeasures mommy-to-be's cervix and, studying E's gasping, doubled-over frame like a connoisseur of maternal suffering, utters the magic word: epidural.

"Now?" E protests, sitting upright with a grimace. "But I was supposed to see the doctor at six tomorrow, and induce."

Big laugh from Shareesa, who's already picked up the phone. "Induce? Honey, only one thing we gotta induce, we gotta induce this gee-dee pain to go away, so you can save your strength for when you need it."

"You mean—?" E looks up at me, wide-eyed.

"Uh-huh," says Shareesa. "I mean this baby's comin', honey. The ol'-fashioned way. And you gonna have to push."

Before she can expound further, whoever she's holding for on the other end of the line picks up, and Shareesa explains the situation. While she talks, I just kind of hang alongside E, trying to keep my own bubbling panic in check now that the fear is finally showing on her face.

"Daddy's feelin' it, huh?" says Shareesa. (Ready or not, fellas, your presence at the hotbed of birth is license for complete strangers, starting with RNs and hospital floor-waxers, to address you as "Daddy." But not in a nasty, *Ride me, Daddy, right me right out of town!* way. I once had a girlfriend who actually said that. She now makes macramé in Cleveland.)

Just to deepen the spookhouse vibe in the delivery room, a white flash cracks the sky, showing the fingery outline of trees tapping the hospital windows, before another massive clap of thunder. It's the kind of night where you half expect a raven to crash into the glass and turn into Dracula—or a newborn baby, as the case may be.

Despite the special effects, Shareesa hangs up and announces matter of factly that the anesthesiologist is on the way. "And he's a real *hottie.*"

While we wait for the (apparently smokin') professional pain killer to show up, E careens between torso-searing contractions and hushed, excited chitchat. "I can't believe this is happening." And—looking down at herself—"I keep thinking, how can her head fit through there?"

I hold her hand, wipe her brow, whisper whatever I can to help get her though. And generally find a half dozen different ways to be semi-useless, as only a father in a delivery room can be.

The contractions come on hard and fast, now that her cervix has expanded north of seven centimeters. In charges the anesthesiologist, the first male to enter the proceedings in a while. He's a buff, young fellow, kind of astronautish, like all the Lone Star medicos I've met so far. He introduces himself as Tim—*Tim?* Are anesthesiologists not MDs?—who doesn't look a minute over seventeen. Then again, one of the treats of being an OG Dad is that everyone looks about seventeen. Which is fine. I wouldn't mind if he tore in on a skateboard with a Dr. Seuss hat, as long as he knew what he was doing.

In this case, for the occasion, the knockout artist is decked out in snug scrubs that—no other way to put this—seem designed to show off his butt. He proceeds to explain that he's going to "go in through the back" with a tube of fentanyl, then numb the area with Lidocaine.

That said, he arranges his instruments and pharmaceuticals in a tray on the counter, then fills a long needle, attaches it to a tube and, with a flourish, steps to the bed and opens E's gown. Exposing her back to reveal, much to his surprise, a giant tattoo of a galloping horse, done *trompe de l'oeil* fashion. Which I may as well add, was more than a tad alarming the first time I found myself facing it. *You* try performing with *War Horse* charging toward you over your girlfriend's ass crack. (Obviously, I managed. Or we wouldn't be in this pickle.)

E moans some more. Then, clearing his throat and dramatically cracking his knuckles, the pert-buttocked anesthesiologist recovers, douses the horse's head with alcohol, and daintily inserts the needle and tube right in its eye. While I wonder at what kind of wanton savagery must have been inflicted on women in the old days, before technology and insurance companies. (And before insurance savagery.) As if reading my mind, Shareesa pipes up, "In olden times, they used to just tie'em down and gag'em with a pair of lady drawers."

Wow, is all I can reply. But, drug delivery system in place, the adolescent anesthesoid explains that he's going to insert a catheter, "since mommy's going to be completely numb downstairs." Then he shows her how she can control the amount of fentanyl she gets in the IV by just pressing her thumb on the button. The deal is, she can feel the pressure but she won't feel the pain. All in all, not a bad way to go through life.

Soon, E's torture is neutralized. Well, more than neutralized. She's feeling *good.* And the night resumes apace, a nonstop whoosh of thunder, nurses, and bouts of brink-of-the-abyss hysterical laughter. Sort of like being on a lifeboat on stormy seas, except that we're on dry land, and not going anywhere. But who has time for half-baked metaphors? Finally, around 5:00 a.m., E goes pie-eyed, and sits up fast. "Oh... Oh fuck! I think she's coming."

The nurse rings the doctor who, as it happens, is not on call until six in the morning. And it's five now. "That figures," the nurse says with a little eye roll. "She's famous."

"For what?" E and I both blurt at the same time.

"What do you think? For stripping membranes on days when she's not on call. You want her to pull out your little dumpling, you're gonna have to squeeze and keep her in there. I know how to deliver, only if I do, there's gonna be a lot of paperwork. "

"But I feel like I have to push!"

"I know, sweetie. Just pretend you're on an airplane and you need to Number Two, but all the restrooms are occupied. What do you do? You *sque-e-e-eze* that li'l old prairie dog back."

This goes on and on until finally, at five to 6:00 in the morning, the nurse gets Dr. Tiny on the phone. Claps her hands when she hangs up. "No pushing! The cavalry's on the way."

The staff has given me damp cloth duty, and I feel, as Norman Mailer once described being a screenwriter in Hollywood, like the towelboy in a whorehouse. Given some kind of ersatz task just cause I'm there and I'm also incompetent. If I weren't doing something, I'd be eating my arms up to the elbows and spinning in circles.

A few more hours till blastoff. But—mind-exploding as that fact may be, there's something else tugging at my psyche. Namely—be still my heart!—the perky male anesthesiologist has excused himself, and left the drug tray sitting on the counter three feet from me. No big deal, of course. For a normal person. But listen: I'm sitting here staring at a fucking narco- candy store: ampules of fentanyl, wrapped syringes, jars labeled Norco, Percocet, and even—god help us, ampules of E's new best friend, oxytocin. This may not mean anything to you. But if you're me, a guy who used to open strangers medicine cabinets even if I had to crawl through their laundry room window and down the hall when they were sleeping to get to them…well, hey, it counts for something. Last time I found myself in the delivery room, I'd laid in Mexican tar and geezed five minutes before I cut my First Daughter's umbilical. Fast forward two decades and change, and I'm back in the baby factory, staring at a veritable opiate smorgasbord, with a love hormone and lidocaine garnish. And I don't go near any of it. (Well, that's not true, I kind of eyeball the stuff.)

Mind you, I'm not looking for a medal here. I haven't shot dope since Bill introduced Monica to cigar-play, but still… I'm fried, it's five in the morning, I've been here since around eight in the evening. This could, under different circumstances, pack all the ingredients of a spectacular relapse. *"Well, see, I was waiting for my child to be born, and it's like the Lord just said "Son, you've been such a good boy, you deserve a couple pops of fentanyl…"* Because dope, make no mistake, will talk to you. Which you either understand or you don't. (And if you don't, god bless and drive safely.) The trick is knowing when to listen and when to shut the voices down. And, thank you, Yahweh, it was more a weird mental side trip, a non-narcotic narcotic meditation, if you will, than an actual *thing*. I skipped the party tray. But the one second vacillation, I won't lie, left me a little quivery.

But what the fuck am I doing? There's a baby coming. And, one thing about newborns, they're the ultimate cure for self-obsession. As mine is proving even before she actually hits the landing strip. Right now, as a matter of fact, things are kicking into high gear. Much hustle & bustle as the pro baby staff swings into action. Much as I hate to sound all mid-career Andy Rooney, but these tubes remind me of the last time I took my ten-year-old Caddy husk in for smog test. And yet, for all the gear, I recently saw on a supermarket headline crawl that the US ranks twenty-ninth in infant mortality. Worse than Slovakia, but—big high five!—better than Bulgaria. And fuck those Slovakians anyway.

•　　•　　•

HAPPILY, THE WOMAN OF the hour, Dr. Tiny, scampers in before E lets go and shoots the fetus against the wall. Planted between the pair of massive, and massively competent, ladies handing the proceeding thus far, our pint-sized OB/GYN looks like a little girl who's wandered in wearing mommy's grown-up clothes. If mommy wore scrubs and knew her way around a delivery room instrument table.

"So how do you feel?" chirps the doctor, laying a strip of plastic on the floor and tugging on a pair of tiny OR booties. For some reason, it's the booties that terrify me.

E's gasps come out pinched. "1…can't… hold it…"

"Perfect! Let's get those stirrups on." And, like *that*, out of nowhere, a pair of what look like leg braces—the kind the kids in my grade school with polio had to wear, but mounted horizontally—flank E's bed like forbidding metal wings.

Now the doctor, an alarming grin on her face, plunges her hands between E's raised and spread legs. Sweat beads on E's forehead. I'm standing at my post mopping it when the doctor glances over at me and winks. "Oh yeah… This baby's just hanging out… She's saying, 'I dig it in here. The food's great… But damn, no free cable!' Oh yeah…she's *close*… "

"It's… It feels too big!" E cries.

"We talked about this," the doctor says, her tone so calming I wonder if she's on oxytocin, or if they teach that calm, seventies FM disc jockey intonation in Delivery School. "She's not that big. And skin stretches. Especially the vagina. If we need to cut to get the baby out, we make a laceration at the point of the skin where you wipe your ass when you go to the bathroom."

"Oh Jesus!" I hear myself groan, without knowing I was going to.

"Will I—" E manages, swallowing hard, "will I need stitching?"

I catch the nurses sneaking glances at each other.

"Depends. First degree lacerations you don't need to stitch. It's like scraping your knee. Second degree, we may have to—"

"*Ewfff…*"

E squeaks in anguish and the Dr. House session squeals to a halt.

"Okay, listen. What I want you to do is put your hands underneath your thighs, legs wide. All right?"

"All right."

E's legs are already up in the stirrups. (But not the stirrups she's used to—the ones on the back of thoroughbreds. It's going to be a while since she straddles anything more challenging than a toilet bowl.)

"Good," the doctor continues, ever calmly. "Now fill your lungs to the top and, without making any noise, I want you to push as hard as you can, just like you're making a bowel movement... Okay, *Push!... Beautiful!*"

I'm at my post, by the head of the bed, mopping E's brow with a weirdly scrapey washrag. The doctor glances up at me. "*Here she comes!* Come on, Daddy, do you want to see?"

And without thinking, I leave the head of the bed and stagger to the foot, where, before I can blink, I see some kind of long black probe protruding from E's savaged vagina. "Jesus fuck! What *is* that? An antenna!?"

E's eyes blaze in my direction. But the doctor finds me hilarious. "That's her hair, silly. She's got a *lot* of hair. That's just a big old curl. "

She's right! For one freakish minute I'm afraid we're going to give birth to the Bob's Big Boy logo. But quick as the spooky probe appeared, it recedes. After which, following a second *"PUSH!"* from the doctor and vein-popping effort from E, what looks like an avocado emerges, then it too disappears again.

The phrase turtlehead comes to mind, and I want to douse my brain with lighter fluid and strike a match as soon as I think it.

"Whoops!" the doctor chuckles. (Talk about grace under pressure! This woman is absolutely giddy with calm.) She smiles up at E, whose face by now is so red I'm afraid she's going to burst and go flying around the room backwards. "We saw her little keppie in there, but she wants to chillax for a while, so just hang for a sec."

I try not to stare, but Jesus! I mean—you don't hear people talk about this, but *come on!*—it's like suddenly I've got Jack Nicholson tickets, courtside at the open vagina playoffs, gawking directly between my girlfriend's befouled and betadined inner thighs. Her, as they used to say in vintage erotica, "exposed womanhood." And what's amazing, I'm sorry, is how quickly this particular anatomical arena, which exists, under normal circumstances, as what our Australian brethren refer to 'the temple of low men"—hot porno action central—how quickly it morphs into something else altogether... A kind of agony pita pocket, source of the love of your life's pain. The act of birth, through some Blakean alchemy, transforms nasty-raw into primal-mysterious. H. P. Lovecraft meets the Marquis de Sade, by way of the Discovery Channel. Still eye-scorchingly riveting—but for entirely different reasons. No longer the X-rated wide open-for-biz "show-me-the-pink!" affair which throbs and glistens in most men's heads... But the—pardon my purple prose, I'm describing something purple—wet palpitating heart of life itself.

"Easy, easy, girl..." The doctor, at this point, is like some kind of womb whisperer. Another push—we see dome—and another—dome and a forehead—then, after a bit of internal maneuvering, the doctor stops, suddenly quiet, and announces—more to the nurses than either E or me—that when the baby comes out, E will not be able to hold it. There may be a problem.

And in that moment—in that moment, a jolt of panic nearly buckles my knees. I take E's hand and listen as the doctor continues. "We've got a meconium situation."

"A what?" I don't know if it's me talking or if it's E.

"The baby pooped, and there's a chance she might get some in her mouth on the way out."

Because my reaction to every trauma in life is to make a joke out of it, my first thought is, "Perfect, not even a minute old, and already eating shit. She may have a future in Hollywood." But before I can share this non-witticism, the doctor continues, turning my smart-ass remark to ashes in my mouth.

"This could be bad," Dr. Tiny goes on. "We'll try and suction it. But if some gets in her lungs, I need to take her to the ICU. There's a chance—"

I don't even hear the rest. The stricken look on E's face has obliterated sound. I think of everything I would do to make this moment all right, to make whatever is about to happen happen in a way that leaves this creature— whom I have never met, whom I may, from the sound of things, *never* meet—alive and healthy and screaming and perfect. The phrase "rip my heart out" becomes literal possibility. A swooning panic soaks my clothes and I see the light in E's eyes go on, through refracted tears.

What I want to do is grab the doctor, tell her, "I will give you anything," as though it would matter, make any difference at all. What I do instead is I take E's face in my hands and tell her, with all the conviction I do not have, "Don't worry baby, it's going to be okay."

With that, the doctor demands one final *Push!* And this time she screams through clenched teeth, through the pain of her ripping perineum, the now-gushing blood from her tearing vagina, and out comes this tiny, black-haired, wailing thing, arms flailing, feet kicking, coated in gore, waving her bloody, prune-sized fists like she'll kill anything that tries to get close to her.

And without even seeing what I'm doing I take the scissors when the doctor asks and I do my job. It takes a couple tries. But I cut it. And then the doctor takes her and I'm so scared, and so full of prayers I don't even know how to utter, that when they rush her to the doctor's table in the corner I don't even scream the words now echoing in my head: *Oh my god, she's a fucking pinhead!*

Because, you see, the top of her skull... what can I say? It's so pointy you could use it for the ring toss at a county fair. (Which, I'm afraid, is where she's going to work, when she grows up, if they still have sideshows.) I hold my mud. But seconds later, when the beaming nurse looks at us and says, "We got it... We suctioned her out, she's fine!" and brings this writhing monkey-girl back from the table and places it on E's chest, I mumble to the doctor, in the meekest of voices, the voice you use when you ask a question to which you really do not want to hear the answer, "Um…her head… Is it, you know, going to be like that her whole life?"

And, before she replies, it hits me, for the thousandth time, you can't bargain with the universe. I prayed the kid would be born healthy, and she apparently was. She just happens to have a skull shaped like a tiny bowling pin. Still, I tell myself, if we stick her in a beanie growing up, and she rocks some kind of beehive as a teen, who's gonna know? Maybe by then they'll have lady popes, and she can wear a pope's hat. The doctor, thank Christ, interrupts my fervid cogitating.

"Trust me," she laughs, before peeling off her scrubs and rushing off to attend another routine miracle, "it will go back to normal in three days. It's just from squeezing through the birth canal. In case you've noticed, it's not that big."

At which point, through her tears, and over the baby's now epic wailing, E screams one final time. Only now she's screaming at me, through laughter I can only describe as happily deranged. Delirious with relief. "You fucking idiot!"

Then they let me hold the baby. And I forget everything.

#8:
Big
Dad
Cann

**y
es**

8 Days Old

FIRST TIME AWAY FROM the baby, and the world is a strange new place. Before leaving, I spent an acid-without-the-acid-esque few days contemplating the tiny faux-hawked nipple-sucker perched atop E's monstro breast. (Young N eschewed the right, oddly enough, already a lefty at two days old.) And, call me sentimental, there's nothing but righteous heroin to compare with the rush I got just padding around, newborn propped against my chest-pelt, feeling her 3:00 a.m. screams calm to coos as I talked her through the late night heebie-jeebies, no doubt inspired by the savage, criminal travesty of being plucked from the lush confines of dark womb heaven and thrust into a world of harsh light, bad air, car-horns, and a goodly amount of Lawrence O'Donnell, whose image on the tube, I must gratefully add, seems to chill her right out as surely as my own back-patting promenades around the stamp-sized living room.

The thing is, I've been invited to Cannes. A movie my name's on is showing there. Glam as it sounds, the last thing I want to do is go anywhere. Seriously. When we run out of diapers, I literally tear full-out to the store and back, because I don't want to miss a single action-packed minute of brand new babydom. Go ahead—make carnival with my excitement. I mean, mere hours ago, I actually heard my pride 'n' joy fart for the first time. I'm talking about an eight-day-old with the rectal pipes of a perogee-fed, forty-year-old Milwaukee steamfitter. I'm bustin' my buttons!

E and I discuss the trip. (Which is new for me. In previous relationships, "discussion" was code for scream, be screamed at, smash computer, put fist through wall, slam door, and then do something regrettable. But never mind. As Nietzsche said—before, I'm assuming, the whole sleep-with-his-sister-and-get-syphilis thing—"*Many a man fails at original thinking simply because his memory is too good."* But enough out of Nietzsche.) E is all for Cannes. "Go ahead and go, baby, we'll be fine." But, my deepest secret: I'm not worried about them. I'm worried about me.

A little backstory here. See, the first time I experienced the miracle of Dadhood, I was so strung out I would do dope to obliterate the reality that, instead of being with my baby, I was, you know, doing dope. (I'm talking here about Baby Number One, whom I loved, of course, in the same, if more narcotically tainted, fashion I love Baby Number Two.) But, really, does it matter what your reasons are for not being with your newborn? Whether you're hobnobbing with Pepe and Red, at the corner of Balloon and Eightball, or with Nicole and Clive on the Riviera, absence is absence. It's not like any of this is rational.

That's why I'm on the fence about the trip. More or less super-glued. Until, when Baby N finally stops wailing and passes out with a wanton gurgle on her evening nipple-snack— left, as mentioned—E shrugs and marches out her position. "Look at it this way, no matter what you decide, on some level, you're going to regret it. So you might as well fucking relax…"

So… Here I am, in an airy seaside verandah in the Palais, the glitzy middle of Cannes, watching people be famous while I kill time until the film I seem to have my name on actually screens, and I can bask in whatever refracted magic actually makes its way to the writer.

Later I'll be strolling the red carpet, photographed as the shorter, more mortal human between Nicole Kidman and Clive Owen. (They're both well over my measly six-foot-nothing.) Not, needless to say, my usual scene… But one, I suppose, which at some point would have been the thrilling highlight to…something. Anyway, right now it's lunch time.

The Big Names on-hand are chowing down at a tanker-sized table, while I'm lurking in the corner, albeit on a sofa so lush I have to fight the urge to go face-down and sleep off jetlag. (That's right, it's the megastar high school lunchroom—and I'm the new kid with thalidomide arms and acne!) Actually I gave my seat up to Bernardo Bertolucci, who, no longer mobile, chugged up to the Big Name table in a Hoveround and kind of parked behind me until, succumbing to guilt at the eyes of the Italian directorial giant boring holes in my occiput, I let him take my parking spot and skulk off to the outer circle of the VIP feeding trough.

Which, in point of fact, is fine with me. I think a lot of writers are corner lurkers. (You've got your Hemingways and you've got your Kafkas, and at the moment I'm feeling Gregor Samsa-adjacent—if Gregor Samsa ever scuttled to the South of France.)

Anyway, I'm over here having a one man lurkathon, weighing down furniture already sagging from collective bodyguard bulk. Hunkered on either side are assorted versions of Jean-Claude Van Damme, speaking French and all, at least in my febrile imagination, discussing *les steroids.* Though perhaps the subject is lobster bisque recipes. My French is spotty.

Physically I'm at Cannes, but all I can think about is the squiggly frog with the fauxhawk. Instead of starstruck, I'm babystruck. Sitting here wondering if Mrs. Binkelstein, at the ripe age of nine days, has learned to roll over or speed dial, and I have—however inadvertently—stuck her with a lifetime of abandonment issues. (We've taken to calling her Mrs. Binkelstein, by the way, because her face, in moments of diaper-filling high dudgeon, resembles that of a disapproving yenta with a bulging bottom lip, crinkly forehead, and the general air of an over-seventy bubby about to look you up and down and mutter, *"Feh!"*)

Call it the post-birth bifurcated psyche. Half of you is wherever you actually are, half of you is elsewhere, astral-neurotically projected into Baby-Obsessoland... I've gone from baby sleep deprived to celebrity jet lagged, chomping pink ravioli while surveying the varying nosh techniques of everyone from Macy Gray (dainty) to semi-old pal Benicio del Toro (no-nonsense) to Tim Roth (laid back) to Matthew Maconnaheydude (you guess). My biggest thrill is meeting director Gaspar Noe (after mistaking him for stubbly bald comedy demigod Dave Atell) whose *Enter The Void* may be the single most intense, beautiful, and disturbingly hallucinogenic mind-fuck-supreme movie ever made. A bit of cinema which, if you haven't seen it, you should stop whatever meaningless activity you're engaged in (including reading this) and procure immediately. It may not change your life, but it will change your brain chemistry. Though not, I suppose, as much as holding a drooly-cute newborn on your chest. Apparently, that really does give you a serotonin blast—and without the headache of a Lexapro prescription. (I've got nothing against antidepressants, but when I tried them, all I got was dry-mouth and insomnia—not to mention my dick morphed into a dog toy. Go fetch!)

The whole look-ma-I'm-in-a-tuxedo, red carpet experience does not kick in until, jammed in the limo (actually some breed of 2015 Mercedes SUV), crawling through the throngs lining the street from hotel to theater, I stare out the tinted glass and catch the eyes of the screamers lining the road. Whatever's fueling their ardor, it is certainly not slaked when, instead of, say, Brad Pitt emerging when the driver opens the door, it's some writer-guy with questionable teeth and a shiny black suit he last wore to court for reasons too sordid and obscure to revisit.

This, for me, is the takeaway of the carpetwalk. Not the unchecked, ungodly awe of the superstar hungry crowd—but its savage, rarely glimpsed opposite: their palpable disappointment when, after standing for hours in the Mediterranean sun, some Jim-Jim McNoname staggers from the star-mobile. I rode over with legendary editor Walter *Apocalypse Now* & *Godfather* Murch and his wife, and believe me, the mob was not happy to see any of us.

Insane as it sounds, at that moment, I actually feel guilty at not being a *People* cover-worthy human. Happily, Clive Owen and Nicole rolled up shortly thereafter. We shoot the shit before the madness commences. Clive's a great laugher. Nicole, despite a gown worth more than my house, is down-home as a second cousin. And, yes, when my pal the director, Philip Kaufman, mentions I'm "a new Papa" I do, with a minimum of nudging, bust out the blackberry and show them a baby photo. I've become *that* guy. Our baby-bonding over, the security pros on hand—some of whom I recognize from the buffet couch—gently (but firmly) hold me back by my wrists as Nicole, Clive, and Phil go on ahead into the maw. (The director, by the way, is an athletic seventy-plusser with a full head of silver hair. Which I mention why? Because, what happens, after you hit fifty, is that you start looking for, not role models exactly, but examples of OGD-types who have braved the wilds of seniordom with the dignity and cool intact. Like Burroughs, or Beckett, or Shecky Greene—guys who wear their survival, as they say, like a loose garment. These giants are a great antidote to the *alta kockers* at my local Y, the old lions whose ear hair could scrape the rust off pieplates and whose balls hang down to their arthritic knees. But where was I?)

Flashbulbs pop like dying brain cells. The stars face the legion to the right, waving and smiling, then the left, more waving, more smiling. Then the nearest Van Damme gives me the nod and, hand pressed to the small of my back, urges me forward. The word surreal does not cover it. It's not even a dream come true, more just a dream: except instead of waking up with no pants in front of my high school algebra class, I'm wide-eyed in a tuxedo—(or faux-edo: black suit, white shirt, and snap-on bowtie) on the Jungian archetypal red carpet—think long uncurled tongue!—in front of a small village of screaming fame-iacs at Cannes.

For a beat, sandwiched between movie stars, I accidentally raise my eyes and catch my own dentally-challenged mug projected on the live screen mounted over the entrance. Clive looks over and laughs. None of this means anything, but still… It's not just unlikely (you're talking to a guy who would, in his former life, have tried to steal the carpet and trade it for a dime bag.) It is, as Hemingway liked to say, a perfect moment. Though all I can think about is how the pictures will be fun to show my little girl, when she's old enough. Or if, years from now in therapy, she wants to show Dr. Clawhammer how her Dad bailed on her eights days after she left the womb. (Rule Number One of parenting: don't project your guilt and weirdness onto your own children. Just in case, I'm going to lay in a couple of autographed photos from the stars, both signed *To the cutest goddamn baby in the world… Your Daddy loves you, even if he has no sense of priorities what-so-fuckingever!* Just so she knows I was thinking about her.)

#9:
Lick
the S
and I

ofa

Die

20 Days Old

MY NIGGLING FEAR, AS a late-in-the-game Dad, was that somehow I'd end up in diapers before my baby was out of them. (The title of this nightmare is *Two in Diapers!—The story of an older gentlemen and his li'l newborn as together they head to Costco for discount disposables.*) Irrational, I know. But so is life. Which is why I should not have been surprised when, after the arrival of our little Pampers-stuffer, this semi-tormenting vision was actually made flesh. Only—weirdly enough—not by me, and not so tormenting. Instead, one special morning I looked up in time to see my girlfriend, still freshly savaged from the happy pain chamber known as the delivery room, step into the bedroom, hoist up her Honk If You Love Satan T-shirt, and shriek, "Check it out!"

With that, she let loose the kind of cackle only sleep-deprived moms and Charles Manson can get away with, then flashed what—for lack of a better term—can only be described as the jumbo mega-nappy she was wearing right in my face.

Seriously. I still remember the shock: staring at a package bigger than Johnny Wadd's—there's a visual!—product of the ice pack and industrial-sized feminine napkin she was forced to rock between her legs as a result of the twenty-five-stitch post-birth taint damage.

Happily, the wounds are healing nicely— slightly faster than my psyche—enough so the New Mom can get back on the horse (literally) and ride for a couple of hours. And, trust me, horse-riding is not a genital region-friendly experience. I've had no taint stitches whatsoever, yet the one time she got my sorry white ass up on a nag and smacked it on the flank, I felt like I was being rabbit punched by a ball-hating hobbit until the thing stopped trotting. (My own taint, thanks for asking, was probably black and blue for a week, though there's no way to make that official without a hand-mirror and pulleys, and I'm not that mechanical.)

Back in babyland, I'm struck by how insanely fast our little space invader seems to have grown. It's as if someone stuck a bicycle pump in her sweet little ear and started pumping. Her head, which started off tiny and pointed, has morphed into spherical perfection, and her hair, already plentiful at birth, has grown out in a full-on, old school Wendy O. Williams mohawk. I would have adored her anyway, but that wet-finger-in-a-socket haircut—Jesus!

I have, I realize, missed half her life—having been off to LA, New York, and Cannes trying to remain a going concern and finance this little wonder-nugget. I left on Day Eight and returned on Day Twenty. This, no way around, makes me kind of an absentee father. Nothing, however, will roll up the red carpet faster than that first splash of tot-vomit when you pick up your little bundle of joy. (Or bundle of goy, in this case, since I'm purebred East Coast bagel and mom's the Southern blonde. One wrong move, and this child will grow up serving deep fried lox.)

Needless to say, I'm in heaven, hanging out with Mother and Child. Listening to the maternal nothings my girlfriend whispers in our little one's ear. Like just now, as she's suckling young Binkelstein, I can't help but eavesdrop: *"You little monkey! I'd love you a lot more, if you didn't keep kicking me in the tit."* Talk about life-affirming! It's almost as good as watching her, in nothing but bulging diaper and flip-flops, using one hand to breast feed baby while swatting Texas-sized flies into bloody mist with the other. (How this is sexy, I'll leave to Dr. Freud—or Dr. Ruth—but why question a good time?) Of all the gifts I've given the mother of my child, none has made her as happy as this flyswatter. Flies are the bane of her existence. I think she'd have actually preferred a .22, but it's a small apartment, and there's always the danger of ricochet.

Anyway… Everything was pretty much aces until I made the mistake of picking up a copy of *The New York Times* that was propping up a flea market chair in our living room. Then—goodbye piece of mind, hello domestic terror—I read an old Nicholas Kristof column, "Are You Safe on That Sofa?" And life has never been the same. I mean, I know our homes are no longer our friends, that toxic killers lurk in every corner, and that Monsanto has probably destroyed more lives than Bin Laden, The Taliban, and Scott Walker combined. But still, when I read about the unregulated flame retardant tris that coats my couch—result of an arcane congressional money slog that starts with the tobacco lobby and ends with gusts of PCB-adjacent petrochemical helldust puffing out of the sofa and causing everything from lower IQ to diabetes to god knows what kind of toddler cancer—that was it.

Thanks to deregulation, a massively uncontrolled carcinogen—think of it as At Home Agent Orange—was even used in nursing pillows, the manufacturers of which were under no compunction to even mention that the stuff was an ingredient. Having purchased both a nursing pillow *and* a new sofa—on which, it gives me hives to admit, I proudly ensconced mom-to-be while awaiting for her water to break—I find myself sitting here wondering when, exactly, the medical anomalies will start to show. *"We're not exactly sure why your little girl's developed brain goiters and umbrella jaw, Mister Stahl. Did you by any chance purchase a sofa when she was in the womb...?"* (And thanks to "tort reform," right wing-ese for "You're fucked," we couldn't sue if we wanted.)

Toxic post-womb medical problem-wise, it's a goddamn jungle in here. And I haven't even mentioned Johnson & Johnson's beloved baby shampoo. Their slogan is "No More Tears!" which features the ever popular tot-fucking chemical combo, 1.4-dioxane, your friendly neighborhood "likely carcinogen," along with quaternium-15, a chemical that releases the preservative formaldehyde. So, basically it's no more tears—until the day your kid starts belching embalming fluid and burns your eyebrows off. But then, you're the one who'll be crying, so the slogan still works.

Not to go all crypto-Luddite here, but holy moly! Once you have a newborn—the most innocent, needy, ridiculously vulnerable creature in the world—it's impossible to escape the sense that to live in twenty-first-century America is to occupy some kind of boundaryless biosphere of corporate death-fumes and profit-driven child-sliming side effects. But unlike, say, Obama's kill list—forever targeting the Number Two Man in Al Qaeda, an organization which seems, oddly, like those Hollywood vanity production companies where everybody is listed as "Vice President"—it's impossible to know precisely who to target for the Carnival

of Cancer into which all American babies are—
ready or not!—aimed and fired.

Don't get me started with the other possible
side effects, like the one that makes girl babies
grow up and start menstruating at eight.
Apparently pediatricians are seeing more of these
all the time. (Probably the hormones in milk. But
I'm still not going to let toxic loveseats off the
hook.) Whatever, the prospect of my daughter
being raped by some pedophile freak, dropping
out to give birth in third grade after being denied
an abortion thanks to President Romney, then
becoming a grandmother at fifteen, after the
same thing happens to her kid, and the two of
them have to take jobs to pay for childcare—
more potential drippage from a government-
shrinking Republican tomorrow… it's all just
too heinous to contemplate. (I can already hear
Foster Friess, crackpot Tea Party zillionaire and
Santorum booster—Remember the Santorum
campaign? Feels like centuries ago!—advising
little girls to put gummy bears between their
knees if they don't want to get pregnant.)

Then again, it's not like *everything* in
America is bad. I'm thrilled that we have enough
food for sixty percent of US babies to grow up
obese. Speaking of which, is it a rumor that

Burger King has started a Hoveround drive-through lane in Alabama, for the convenience-minded too-big-to-get-out-of-a-chair crowd? If so, forget Facebook—put your money in electric wheelchairs and retire young. That's what I'd like to do. Except for the fact that I'm too old to either die young or retire that way. Plus. which, if I didn't have writing to keep me busy, I'd be off tracking down household toxin-foisting, child development-compromising lobbyists and Congressmen. Sneaking, say, into the home of Andrew Liveris, CEO of Dow, the world's largest manufacturer of tris, then dragging him back to my house to lick my couch at gunpoint until his eyes bleed and tumors sprout in his brainpan like toadstools after rain. Not that any of this will make my child any safer. But it might make Daddy happy. And everybody knows a chipper parent makes for a chipper baby.

#10:
Milk-
aholi

C

43 Days Old

I T's BEEN FORTY-THREE DAYS since Baby N came in for landing. Maybe too early to wax sentimental, but not, I hope, to revisit the particular weirdness of Mondo Maternito. On the heartstrings, man-enough-to-tear-up side, there's the memory of how, seconds after birth, I placed my pinkie in my daughter's hand and she wrapped her fingers around it. As if to say, "I have no idea how I fucking got here, but is it okay if I hang on?" And how, a minute after that, the RN slapped her in an ankle bracelet, like a low-level felon under house arrest. We were told that if we got within five feet of any of the exits, including elevators, alarms would go off.

I *had* wondered why there were uniformed policemen posted everywhere. Was all the security necessary? At that age—and by age I mean, like, nine minutes old—babies can't even crawl. So what were they going to do? Poop their way to freedom? Why the tiny fascist hardware? The cops sat outside the same rooms every night and every day, for the three days I was in there. Mind you, I'm not even talking about the undercovers tricked out, no doubt, as pregnant women and, for all I know, babies—tiny mewling UCs, keeping an eye on the surroundings to make sure no one escaped. I figured the authorities allowed some convict to visit his newborn, and his handlers waited outside to make sure they didn't make a run for it. That, or some *America's Most Wanted*-type with a vagina had given birth, and they wanted to keep her on lockdown. Before deciding whether to give the baby to Social Services, Grandma, or Angelina Jolie.

Turns out I had it all wrong. They weren't keeping the babies from escaping. They were keeping strangers from coming in and escaping with babies. Less than a month earlier, our nurse explained, a Texas woman tried to grab somebody else's newborn and make it her own. Apparently her own had been lost in a miscarriage. A truly heartbreaking and made-for-Lifetime crime.

Whose commission, apparently, resulted in Baby Ward vigilance. And in retrospect it's good to know how vigilant. They've wiped out Planned Parenthood in Texas. So mothers don't have to worry about wasting time with prenatal care or abortions. They can just hunker down and wait till it's time to enter whatever obstetric Fort Knox they find to snip their umbilical and send them on their way.

The postnatal lockdown was a bit of a jolt. But nothing compared to the of sight of my baby's anatomy. Nobody told me, going in, that baby girls are born with genitals as pink and protruding as Nature Channel orangutan ass. I mean, they could have warned me first! For one bad minute, I thought my girlfriend may have been consorting with a hot primate.

These are the kind of happy memories that bounce around a guy's brainpan after his six-week-old scoop of ice cream has been yowling nonstop for four or five hours. I'm spotting for E, who keeled over with a haunted look and plaintive plea to "please take over" what feels like a week ago.

Side note: when we left the hospital, seventy-two hours after the birth of Binkelstein, we were both kind of amused and creeped out by the thick stack of papers the staff stuck in our hands on the way out the door—at least half of which dealt with the subjects of "depression and anger," specifically the kind of anger that makes you want to "shake your baby." Included, along with the hotline numbers, are a variety of tips for dealing with this, apparently—and sadly, all too common urge. "Take a few deep breaths…remember something that made you happy!" The ludicrousness of which, I have to say, you really can't appreciate until you've been subjected to that ceaseless, brain-stabbing, accusatory squall yourself. Having been in Scream Therapy for a while now, I have to wonder why the ATF blasted nonstop Metallica down there in Waco, back when David Koresh was holed up with his Branch Davidian followers. If the fibbies had just subjected them to a night or three of quadrophonic wailing infants, the whole sect would have run weeping out of the house, and the government could have avoided all the troublesome paperwork that comes with burning seventy-one men, women, and children to death.

Tonight, our little Klaus Nomi started in around 2:00, and *Democracy Now*—which comes on at 6:00—is just about wrapping. Amy Goodman's been interviewing Jeff Masters, director of meteorology at the Weather

Underground website, discussing rampant fires, heat waves, and water wars, guaranteed staples of the future Baby N will inhabit. The future I inflicted on her. The Weather Underground is a group of progressive meteorologists who want the weather media to start mentioning global climate change, instead of fluffing the public with record heat wave stats, like global warming is some kind of Olympic event, and we're all cheering for another broken record. *Why, folks, this is the hottest day in Washington since Dick Morris broke his tooth on a hooker's toenail in 2007!* Meteorologists like Masters believe their fellow weathermen have a moral obligation to discuss not just the effects, but the environmental causes, of the new Toast Age we seem to be entering.

Normally, these brutal previews of Life on Planet Hotplate depress the shit out of me. Well, in all honesty, they do now. Before my First Daughter was born, I'm not proud to admit, I used to secretly savor details of the sizzling dystopia to come—the more grisly the better. *By 2050, most human beings will forced to crawl on their hands and knees in the dark and snort guano!* What the hell? I'll be well out of it. Once I had some skin in the game—in the form of a child for whose well-being I would eat my own face—all bets were off.

This morning, however, not even news of Inferno America can penetrate the aural fortress of doom in which Baby N's vocal reaming has locked my skull. Talk about your *cri de coeur*! After three minutes my eyes water, after three hours my ears are bleeding. If she's this inconsolable at a month and a half, I can't help but think, what's the rest of her life going to be? (I almost said she makes Yoko Ono sound like Doris Day, but only old fucks—who aren't necessarily dads—know who Doris Day is. Though a certain kind of obsessive old fuck will know that her son, record producer Terry Melcher, was pals with Charlie Manson. Dennis Wilson, of Beach Boy fame, brought Charlie by Terry's house at 10050 Cielo Drive to play some tunes, in hopes Doris's pride and joy would want to produce a Manson album. Terry passed. But by the time Charlie sent his Family out to 10050 Cielo Drive to make Terry pay for his taste, Melcher'd moved out and Sharon Tate had moved in. The rest is history. Some say Hitler started the Holocaust cause nobody liked his watercolors. Roman Polanski might be an Old Grand-Dad today if Doris Day's baby boy had only liked Charlie's singing. Then again, maybe it's just that Mama Manson never breast-fed her pre-swastika'd toddler.) *Que sera sera.*

Worse than our dumpling's heart-searing vocals, however, is the little Pain Hula that goes with it. Bink's arms kind of flare from her sides, straight for the ceiling. Then she uncurls her fists, bangs open the preternaturally long fingers she inherited from her mother as though throwing two-handed craps. (As opposed to taking them, Huggie-filling being part of the newborn's job description; which is a whole other bag of diaper candy.) All accompanied with out-thrust indignant lower lip and tear-filled *how-could-you-be-so-uncaring-and-horrible* eyes. At that age, tears don't actually roll down their cheeks, their eyes just fill up, which somehow is even more poignant. Her message is clear: *I am in deep and inexplicable pain here! Do something! What kind of incompetent, loser parents are you?!* Is six weeks too young for existential angst? Was Camus a crybaby?

If, like me, you came up in a screamy household, you may have a special vulnerability to the sound of another human being railing at you. When the human being weighs less than a pair of bundt cakes, and you love them enough to sacrifice your entire being—beginning with your sanity, peace of mind, sleep hygiene, and will to live, in no particular order—the effect is devastating. Until you learn some kind of

detachment—and where do they teach that?—
it's like having your soul deep fried and your
thoughts scrambled every night.

If, also like me, you're genetically possessed
of a strain of guilt immune to logic or Dr.
Spock—the famed baby shrink Nixonites
blamed for sixties-era "permissiveness" (i.e.
hippies), not the Vulcan—you will likely feel
responsible for the desperate yelps emanating
from your child.

Happily, there is a solution. Milk. All babies
are milk junkies. That first taste of Mommy
juice kicks in a high that has my daughter
nodding and drooly within a millisecond of her
first hit. If you don't believe me, stand there and
watch a screaming toddler's eyes roll back in
their head while they goes limp in the grips of
milk bliss. As an ex-heroin professional, I'd be
lying if I did not admit I'm slightly (and semi-
embarrassingly) jealous every time I witness
my little girl satisfy her cravings. When my
First Daughter was doing the very same thing,
I was actually still shooting dope. Even then it
weirded me out how all of us are basically born
addicted. Living from tit-rush to tit-rush, with
a lot of nodding off, puking, and howling in
between.

I'm not talking just about out-of-the-womb junkies, or crack babies. I'm talking about you, little newcomer. Just the way He, She, or It made you.

And there it is. *I'm Baby N and I'm a milkaholic…* Or, as her mother likes to say, "I'm more than a mom, I'm a minibar."

Needless to say, I am hardly the first person in the world to notice that babies are hope-to-die milk drunks. My late friend Hubert Selby used to talk about the Sugar Tit. How addicts were toddlers who didn't get the pleasure medicine they wanted, when they wanted it. Or maybe they were born so extra sensitive they needed it more than regular babies—which kept them babies. *The world is just too much, man!* Either way, as adult lushes and druggies they could do what they couldn't do as infants: control the flow. Because, to quote The Hokey Pokey, that's what it's all about. Control. Babies don't have any. So they scream. Some of us still do; some—occasionally—just want to. Selby used to describe himself as "a scream looking for a mouth."

The amazing thing, to me, is that we ever stop.

#11:
How
Depre
a Ba

to

ess

by

IDEAS, AS FAMED VEGETARIAN and human breast milk fan, George Bernard Shaw, once said, are not responsible for the people who embrace them. Sucklin' George got him some nipple every day, and lived to a ripe ninety-five. But—case in point—guess how thrilled Shaw was when the most famous vegetarian of his generation turned out to be, not Shaw, but Adolf Hitler?

(My own breast milk experience, thus far in Old Guy Dadhood, does not involve ingesting. Though I did, one groggy night in July, nearly lose an eye when E had a pap mishap and shot a 1963 Alabama National Guard firehose-level blast of mother's milk directly into my unibrow. Three centimeters left or right and I'd be sporting a patch and turning in my driver's license. Instead I just wiped and went back to diapering. Which may be just as well.)[1]

Then there's Rush Limbaugh, aka America's Keith Richards.

I have no idea if Rush is a fan of Mom-Dairy. From the look of those womanly hips— no disrespect, Big Fella!—more likely mom-butterfat. But, thanks to a well-publicized, huge-enough-to-destroy-his-hearing OxyContin habit, Rush has become, front and center, the pasty face of contemporary drug addiction, here in the USA. Right up there with contempo narco-poster children like Whitney and Kurt. What's not to be proud of?[2]

Had Limbaugh been top dog Dope Icon when I started shooting, I would have steered clear of the stuff and stuck to boilermakers. Dope was much cooler when spokes-junkies like Keith and Jimi, not to mention Lenny,

1   These days, breast-feeding packs its own potential tragedy. If I may quote from M.G. Lord's excellent review of Florence Williams life-changing work, *Breasts*, in the September 16, 2012 *New York Times Book Review*. "The practice also typically transfers 'paint thinners, dry-cleaning fluids, wood preservatives, toilet deodorizers, cosmetic additives, gasoline by-products, rocket fuel, termite poisons, fungicides, and varieties of flame retardants, one of which, Penta-BDE, was banned by the European Union because of its chronic toxicity to humans."

2   Fun fact! Rush isn't the first fatass, fascist, opiate addict to leave titanic skidmarks on the skivvies of Western Civilization. That distinction goes to—what are the odds?—another Nazi: Hermann Goering.

Billie, Miles, and bouncing Bill Burroughs, were the ones in the phone book when you looked up addict. But Rush? Give me a double methadone, three bear claws, and a Narcan back. I've said it before, but Drug Czar Gil Kerlikowske should give the man a medal for making painkillers repulsive. (Imagine how Jesus would feel if He had to listen to Christian rock!) Again—Repetition of Theme-alert!— ideas aren't responsible for the people who lame-ify them. (Other case in point: Walmart, who happens to the biggest corporate user of solar power, and is, even as we shriek, the subject of a strike by warehouse workers in Riverside, California, who, for eight dollars an hour, work in buildings as hot as 110 degrees inside, with either no water or water provided by bosses and described by workers as "foul and full of debris." Braving ninety-five degree heat—outside— workers opted to make a fifty-mile march to Los Angeles to call attention to their plight, which has been largely ignored in the media obsession with the bold and world-changing 2012 elections. And, yes, Michelle Obama *has* decided to partner with Walmart, whose board have actively supported her antiobesity campaign. Presumably, establishing oven-like

Middle Passage warehouse conditions, Walmart will help employees shed unwanted pounds.)

All right then. It was a long way around, but there's a point in sight. I have come to discover that Shaw's theory applies to fatherhood. Deep as I am in Show Business Denial, there's still no way to hide from the fact that every other movie and TV show dropping wet and slick from the curdled loins of Hollywood involves a human being with male genitals and his relationship to his recent newborn. One stellar recent example being ABC Family's *Baby Daddy*. Whose promo describes it thusly: *Ben becomes a surprise dad to a baby girl when she's left on his doorstep by an ex-girlfriend. Ben decides to raise the baby with the help of his mother, his brother Danny, his friend Tucker, and Riley the girl who is harboring a secret crush on him.* Talk about TiVo heaven!

Right now I'm watching another network daddy show. *Guys With Kids.* One guy's newly divorced. One guy's the happily married hipster father. And, hot off *Law and Order,* Anthony Anderson crushes it as the stay-at-home dad. He's so tired, he says he gets up in the morning and tries to put his legs in his shirtsleeves.

Comedy gold! Sort of. I mean, I'm not saying it's *Louie.* (CK doesn't use a laugh track.) But what the hell? Just because your idea of fun is doing the Sunday *New York Times* crossword in magic marker, drunk on gin and lighter fluid, doesn't mean you can't enjoy a good Word Find.

No, my problem with the spate of TV pop-coms is not with the jokes and tone. (What do I know, anyway? I'm twice the age of the demographic.)

I can relate to the nonstop fatigue and sleep-deprived dementia. And my baby does cute shit, just like the babies with agents. What fucks with me is what's *not* in the TV version of newborn Daddyhood.

Unlike network wack-a-daddies, I know there's a fucking world outside the one I inhabit with my adorably adorable spawn. I am not, for you cynics, talking about the Big Issues. Like the fact that by the time Baby N is twenty, all natural aquifers on the planet will have been bought up by Monsanto, Nestle, or the Bush family, who may well decide to sell fresh water only to those who can afford them. Making non-fecally challenged bacterial water the H2O equivalent of Cristal for future generations. Or that, thanks to the greenhouse effect increasing mean temperatures by a degree a year, an anomaly like the hantavirus (let's all visit Yosemite!) will become the norm, and those whom the sun has not yet baked into melanomic stress monsters will be huddled in air conditioned hovels, assuming they have power. (Or, for that matter, hovels.)

But hey! Time out from the Eternal Bleak! I have to get up and take a pee. And, I'm not going to lie, whenever I carry my four-month-old little sweetheart into what my mother used to call "the john," I feel like I may be committing some kind of crime against propriety. Standing there, baby in one hand, johnson in the other, relieving myself, I wonder if suddenly copters will begin whirling overhead, Klieg lights suddenly light up my house, and some branch of *Law & Order: SVU* will come sweeping in, so my heinous neighbors will see me led off in infamy by Ice-T. That said, what's a cashew-bladdered Dad supposed to do—leave his little munchkin lying on the carpet to be eaten by the family dog? Happily, I've talked to other dads, and to a man, they all say the same thing: it's not something you'd do with your four, fourteen, or twenty-four-year-old, but hey, a baby's a baby. And yet—this is the fun part—to the man, as well, all dads make sure their baby's head is facing the other direction. I mean, what are we, priests? How insane is that?

But back to serious issues. Am I being Don Depresso here? I don't want to come off like some kind of whining, eco-global panic freak. Thank gosh, there's plenty of local splendor to get worked up over, too. I'll never forget that heady thrill, the first time my First Daughter and I stepped over a homeless sidewalk sleeper on Silver Lake and Sunset. She was maybe one-and-a-half, and I could think of absolutely nothing appropriate to say. Instead, I blurted, *"Hey, somebody else has poopy pants!"* At her age, I wasn't sure she could grok the implications of global outsourcing and then-president Bush's special brand of economics. Her only experience with "trickle-down" was a leaky Huggie. (Cue laugh track.) Instead I gave the guy a dollar and headed on into Café Tropical for our traditional Sunday morning guava pie. (Full disclosure, I also didn't mention that I'd shot dope with the sidewalk recliner a year or so earlier. Our children have a lifetime to be disillusioned about their parents. Why rush?)

•　　•　　•

ANYWAY, FUCK ME. IT'S been a while since I've written a column. For weeks I have wanted to write about the giddy weirdness of hanging with the tiny, fauxhawked newcomer gurgling up at me this very minute, combined with the mind-numbing rage incurred when trying to assemble a Pack'n Play, a singing electric baby swing, and a Joovy three-wheeled jogging stroller. (Not that I jog, but I might take it up.)

We're talking real sitcom fodder. But every time I try to bang out some wacky, device-assembly gag, the gelid, rictus grin of Mitt Romney curdles my psyche, dominating my brain like the giant poster of Orson Welles' jowls in *Citizen Kane*. Heinous trumps lovable, every time. It hits me, inextricably, that Romney, the best friend Monsanto ever had, will use my child's world with all the love and temperance of a rich teenager jerking off in a sock.

But enough about me. Ultimately, too many obscenities abide to became insanely neurotic about any one of them. Maybe the soul crushing secret of twenty-first century post-environmentally inhabitable Planet America is to just…find a way not to think about it. For brief periods of time. To not let the specter of a grotesque future steal the sleepless wonder of whatever babified present you happen to inhabit.

For the past week—by way of explanation—I've been reading the Chris Hedges and Joe Sacco masterpiece, *Days of Destruction, Days of Revolt*, which focuses on what Hedges calls Sacrifice Zones. (The sacrifice, in these cases, going to the Moloch of Capitalism.) The authors take us to Pine Ridge Reservation in Nebraska, where the average life expectancy is forty-eight, one out of every five girls attempts suicide before the end of high school, and the locals spend their days sprawled on the ground guzzling malt liquor, when they can scrounge enough change to buy some. Hedges also writes about Camden, New Jersey, a high-crime, inner-city inferno, whose government can no longer afford a police department. And Welch, West Virginia, where coal companies have blasted off mountain tops, turning the once-lush landscape into a pitted, oozing boil of carcinogenic runoff and poisoned dirt. We're talking about entire towns where residents have lost their gall bladders, along with their loved ones, to the unregulated, unrepentant greed of mine owners.

Hedges' point is that these pockets of unimaginable despair are not grim exceptions. They represent the template for the future of America, in the same way that what was done to Native Americans was the template for what was done to people in the Philippines, Cuba, Vietnam, Iraq, and Afghanistan. Now, as Hedges and Sacco illustrate, "it is finally being done to us."

But forget all that. How cute is my little munchkin when she makes her Liberace face and craps pumpkin pudding? Cuter than George Bernard Shaw with a human milk moustache.

#12:
Inhe:
the V

rit
Vind

4 MONTHS OLD

A BABY IS LIKE a Rorschach. An occasionally adorable, periodically screamy blob onto which we project our own fears, delights, and inner damage.

Or something.

All I know is that last week, for one day, Lil' N refused to smile. Period. She wasn't having it. I'd been away for a couple of weeks, and upon my return, expecting the usual cooey, life-affirming, prelingual love-fest—I mean, why else have a baby?—I got instead the steady, appraising gaze of a bank manager poised to reject my loan application. "And you, sir, you expect me to trust you? *Pray tell why?*" Chilling.

E, of course, being a smart (which is to say not-as-brain-dented-as-me) mother, was more sanguine about our toddler's Sudden Onset Gravitas. "Maybe she doesn't feel like smiling. Do you feel like smiling all the time? You think she's, like, a little 'make life fun for daddy' machine? Is that the deal?"

Tou-fucking-*ché!* Defending a child from genetic paranoia can make any parent testy.

I am mortified. Now that my own behavior is reflected back at me—the true joy of coupledom—I am forced to look at it. Jesus! How could anyone be so solipsistic? So selfish? Somehow, I have managed to let niggling insecurity morph in to unregenerate out-of-control douche-nozzledom.

"You're right," I say. "You're absolutely right!"

And then, three seconds after that, "So, seriously, you think she doesn't like me or what?"

Had E picked up a fire extinguisher and given me a bagel head—hot new trend from Japan!—I would not have blamed her.

The rest of the evening, our child rocked, rode in her jungle-sounds electric swing, rolled in her stroller, woke up from mega-naps, and glared at me during wet diaper changes sans mirth, delight, giggles, or joy. It was like putting a Huggy on Alfred Hitchcock. Minus the theme music.

Another half day of nonsmiling offspring later and I'm crouched by the Pack'n Play, wondering if I have, you know, said something, maybe accidentally insulted young Binkelstein. Babies, any parent will tell you, hate it when you laugh around them. It makes them cry. Especially—and yes, I admit to having done it—if you're laughing at them. They just know. Like say, when there's a loud noise and my tiny daughter twitches and her eyes go wide as a silent movie actor. And I say, "Can you believe how much she looks like Fatty Arbuckle!" And she gets really, righteously indignant.

Forget that four-months-out-of-the-womb humans do not generally understand English. (Plus which, unlike everyone else in America, they don't yet have weight issues. Assuming her first words aren't "Does my ass look fat in this diaper?") Tiny N has a cloud in her eyes that seems to bespeak inner torment, perhaps even existential angst. To the extent that pre-crawlers are, you know, existential. Her lower lip's outthrust, her chin crunched in; tears are welling up. If she knew how, she'd probably be stomping her foot. (Happily, I know from experience, the foot-stomping doesn't start till three.)

And then, suddenly, at the height of my baby's agita, comes an effect straight from vintage Robert Crumb. Rank onomatopoeia. A seat-fluttering *blap*! A fart so loud the bassinet shakes. Books rattle off the shelves and our basenji, Alvin, exchanges a nervous glance with our goldfish, Marv, who flaps his one fin frantically around his bowl. After which, even louder, from south of her diaper-top, comes *blappedda-blap, gurgle-gurgle, blap-blap-ferble-goooosh-sh-sh*!

My thirteen pound squiggler breaks wind worthy of a 300-pound, borscht-fed Ukrainian steamfitter. I know this because my great-uncle Boiny actually was a 300-pound Ukrainian steamfitter. His mother—with whom Uncle Boin-Boin lived until he keeled over from a coronary at fifty-six—never met a meal that couldn't be made better with boiled cabbage. Including breakfast. The result was a digestive tract, in Boiny's case, that can only be described as NASCAR-esque.

Apparently, high-decibel flatulence, like left-handedness and Brillo hair, can skip a few generations. But when it returns, it returns big.

Cue "Here Comes The Sun."

After her baritone sax solo, my little honker smiles with such giggly delight I can't help but pick her up and do a few Hopak dance steps.

(When he got drunk, Uncle Boiny swore he was a Cossack, and the Hopak is the dance Cossacks do when they dance. That thing where guys squat with their arms crossed and kick their legs in and out. Google Yul Brenner. He also liked to climb to the top of his apartment building and get more drunk, guzzling vodka one-handed while swaying on the lip of the roof, reciting verses by Osip Mandelstam. "I am wearied to death with life / There's nothing it has that I want…")

O Osip! I can still hear him!

Mine are a moody, despairing people, pain-stamped by Stalin and Hitler. And most of my female relatives have Moe Howard's nose. My girlfriend's tribe hails from Finnish iron miners. (Though, oddly, even the men are pretty.) I imagine them all, at a wedding party, facing the wall and weeping.

But never mind.

Right now I'm leaning down close to my little girl, on her third-of-a-year birthday, trying to kiss her on her gravity-defying, Wendy O. Williams mohawk, and I'm happy to say she's laughing in my face.

#13:
My Bal
Does tl
Hanky

y

e

Panky

5 Months Old

As if the recent presidential campaign was not disturbing enough, in the middle of it, my five-month-old morphed into Donald Trump. I'm not saying her mother once snuck off to climb Trump Tower when she said she was going out for gelato. It's probably a coincidence that our child looks real estate-ish. All I know is, one day while smearing on organic diaper cream, I looked down, realized Baby N's hair had gone unnaturally red and feral, and noticed the belligerent sneer on her face, a kind of Superior Race lip curl that no one in my family going back to Great-Great-Great-Great Grandpa Shlomo has ever owned.

And just to further twist the whole experience, as Baby N hit the five month mark, she discovered her vagina. Picture if you will, a half-year-old Donald aiming her preternatural smirk your way while gurgling and thrumming her genitalia. Masturbating babies may be the best-kept secret in parenthood. As if, in some unspoken pact of delicacy, moms and dads have decided to keep this quirk of tot-dom to themselves, sensing—quite rightly—that, for those who have never actually witnessed the festive diddling of fresh-out-of-the-oven pleasure seekers it may be just be *too much*. Conceptually.

I once heard progressive talk show giant (giantess?) Randi Rhodes remark that on every birthday her mother reminds her how she was born masturbating. I also just saw Louis CK do a whole riff on the subject of his little girl's labial antics on his HBO special. The whole deal's not unique at all—until you throw in the Donald face.

Naturally, I did what any parent would do when they find their five-month-old cavorting in what Pat Robertson would doubtless refer to as a "highly secular and unholy fashion". I hit the internet. And there it was, in black and white, on BabyCenter.com: "Toddlers masturbate for the same reason that older children do. It feels good."

This, mind you, is not idle patter. It's been verified by the *Baby Center Medical Advisory Board!* The article (titled, catchily enough "Masturbation") continues, quoting nurse practitioner Meg Zweiback—and no, I didn't make it up, perhaps she works at a hospital with Nurse Toll House and Dr. Nutter Butter. Anyway, to quote Nurse Zweiback, "A toddler may masturbate herself to orgasm complete with panting, red face, and a big sigh at the end. But it's absolutely not something to be worried about."

Really? Did baby Jesus do this? I mean, I'm no prude, I don't begrudge a recent newborn a little finger fun. (Though I'll admit, I could have gone the rest of my life without having to process the concept of "tot-gasm.") It's not like a kid that age has much else to do besides suck mommy's nipple, crap herself, and stare out the window at trees. Poor thing can't even crawl, so she can't sneak off for a quickie where no one can see her.

As nature would have it, Baby N's sudden interest in self-stimulation coincides with the discovery of her own voice. She now yammers all day long, raising her eyes to mom and dad like we're a couple of feebs for not being able to understand her inchoate gurps and blurbles.

But that's the thing: maybe it's not gurpling. Watching her work her nether cleft and babbling loudly at the ceiling, how do I know that she's not actually saying something? *That— just thinking this makes me wants to slap oven cleaner on a Q-Tip and jam it into my brain— that she's not actually fantasizing about Justin Bieber and yelping, in some prelingual as yet undeciphered crib-speak: "Oh yeah, Justin, yeah! You're such a dirty little poopy-pants!"*). THE HORROR!

Seriously, I don't know whether to run out the door or text Sally Mann. The whole phenom makes me feel like my head's going to shoot flames. Why don't they tell you this in the hospital before they send you home? Not that it's bad or somehow immoral. (Victorian nannies who believed that masturbation was Satan's work would tie helpless infant's hands to the bars of their crib, like they were wretches in debtor's prison.) At first, I'm not going to lie, the performance was a little…shocking. Doubly so because not two weeks ago, E and I read in the *Times* about the pedophilic New York cop who got caught sending emails full of fantasies about sex with infants, along with *Top Chef* ruminations on the joys of dappling their plump little thighs with butter and roasting them. I couldn't help but imagine that somewhere in a world with enough child-centric perversion to keep *Law & Order: SVU* on the air for fourteen years, some sicko was getting off watching a roomful of Romanian newborns on secret "toddler cams".

"Privacy," Nurse Zweiback goes on to explain, "means nothing to an 'under three.' It's not a meaningful concept." Fair enough. As long as she's not still doing it on subways at thirty, no harm/no foul. But what really is a progressive-minded product of a creepily dysfunctional (don't ask) family to do? Well, thanks again to the No Nonsense Crew at Babycenter.com, my go-to guide for all things parenty and problematic, I know the answer: "Distract her. Even knowing it's normal, even knowing lots of children do it, you'll probably be embarrassed if your toddler starts masturbating in front of company. If you can't ignore it or laugh it off, distraction is your best bet. Masturbation is a lot like nose-picking—children do it because it's there, because they're bored, and because their hands are free. If your toddler's hands stray toward her crotch at inopportune moments (in front of your in-laws, for example), keep a squeaky toy or other substitute handy… anything that keeps her hands out of her pants."

Wow! She had me right to squeaky toy. I'm no Sigmund Freud, but isn't it at least even odds that if I squeak her bunny every time my little sensualist rides the climax train, she might grow up suffering relationship-killing fantasies about rabbits every time she and her love-partner try to have "normal" sex? (The actual syndrome's name is Leporinia, an obsession, generally sexual with actual, artistically rendered, or toy bunnies.) Every Easter will be a living hell until they find a cure. I can only pray that she doesn't grow up and develop a Crush Fetish—trying to block her Peter Rabbit scenarios by snuffing out a store-bought bunny with a pair of six-inch heels. (In Berlin, there are special clubs. *Café Der Hase Töten.*)

But why worry about an uncertain future? Lately Baby N just puts the plushy long-ears in her mouth while slapping her diaper. At six months, she has not yet figured out how to slide her hand into her Huggie and merely smacks it, looking confused that somebody pulled down the garage door.

In other words, she's perfectly normal. Dad's the one who's feeling a little weird.

#14:
Backor
Now

alypse

7 MONTHS OLD

BEFORE WHAT HAPPENED HAPPENED at Sandy Hook Elementary, I was going to write about back pain. Specifically Boomer Back—a dark secret of infant-spawning post-fifty boomerdom—a malady specific to "older parents" forced to bend forward, as if taking a bow, and lift their plump, late-life lollipops out of their cribs. In the last century, crib makers designed their product so the sides of the thing simply folded down. Back before parenting got rebranded as a lifestyle choice (an affectation since replaced by beards), your basic mom or pop did not have to fold at the waist and hoist their little one over the top like some deus ex machina freeing a lifer from his cell in Sing Sing. Back then the 'rents could simply reach in, laterally, and snatch young Tyler or Jessica without bulging a disc and popping a spinal baby bump. In the world of Old Guy fatherhood, it's not just moms-to-be who get a happy bulge; it's post-fifty types with disc issues. (Forgive the digression, but why *do* babies end up behind bars, like tiny, diapered convicts? What are they in for?)

Anyway, due to safety concerns—not, as I first assumed, over a few savvy tots learning to unlatch their cages, bounce onto the linoleum, and make a crawl for it, but 150 tragic deaths by suffocation or strangulation—the CPSC (Consumer Products Safety Commission) eighty-sixed side cribs and opted for top loaders. After which, as my Bentley-driving Beverly Hills sciatica pro informed me, business got very, very good for spine surgeons.

Trust me, nothing makes you feel like a real man like having to ask your 110-pound girlfriend to pick up your toddler for you. But fuck that. A detail like the one above—150 dead babies, due to industry idiocy—rightly drowns out whatever little nugget of kvetchy skaghound bemusement I was going to bang out. Kicks it into grisly foreshadowing of the fact that, in these vicious times, it's what seems safest in life—cribs! schools!—that most often morphs into murderous and unspeakable tragedy. America has its own weird progress: we've expanded our child-killers from factory-made to flesh-and-blood. (In industrial terms the faulty product in question, most recently, being a twenty-year-old still-at-homer who didn't want his picture in the yearbook.)

The grim irony that a prepper mom was preppered for everything but her own son is hard to ignore. In a dark moment, after a day of cable news recaps, I found myself wondering what thought went through the gun-loving mom's head when, woken from sleep, she saw the last thing she would ever see: her own boy—another gun lover!—pointing a Bushmaster at her. Surprise? Terror? Pride? To quote Alexander Pope, in *Moral Essays* (sometimes a guy just has to read a little Pope): "Just as the twig is bent, the tree's inclined." But let us pause, for a moment, to make a note of the name of the product in question. The Bushmaster. Would not, in the deeper recesses of his unconscious, a man with inadequacy issues feel a little buoyed by the notion of *mastering bush*? I'm not going to elaborate.

Okay, okay. If I'm scattered, forgive me. Mass child homicide will do that. Did I already mention that, after my backbone exam at

Cedars Sinai, we had our first appointment with a new pediatrician on the other side of town? The waiting room was divided into a SICK side and a WELL side. (The signs in black crayon, taped up and sagging.) Immediately—and wrongly—assuming the signs were referring to parents' psycho-emotional health, I made for the unwell wing before E grabbed my arm and steered me in the right direction. WELL, happily, was crowded. Kids and mothers, kids and aunts, kids and grandmothers. Only one male beside me. A scowling Asian fellow in an elevator repairman jumpsuit mutters in the corner, tapping a Bic pen on the clipboard as he wrestles with the New Patient Form. *"What am I—trying to get a mortgage here?"*

Two seconds after we meet our new doctor—think smirky Elizabeth Warren, with chunky white orthopedic shoes and forbidding cankles—she launches into a list of seven-month milestones, none of which our child has reached. *Is she crawling? Does she climb the bars of her crib? How much tummy time does she do each day?* By the time the pediatrician finishes her spiel—smirking, it feels to me, sadistically, I feel like I may be raising a tree stump, and wonder if I have to go all *Great Santini* on Bink's under-one-year-old ass. "No need for concern," the pediatrician adds, after I think she's done, "she should advance *eventually*." It's the eventually that makes me cringe. For a second, after the doctor's damned us with our daughter's lack of critical motor skills, I suddenly flash on Andrew Wyeth's trademark painting, *Christina's World,* picturing Baby N, at twenty, dragging her dead legs behind her through the swaying grass, towards the family house on a hill.

Interrupting my brain dive, E snaps back at Dr. Dryenitchy, "She's fine, okay? Every baby grows at their own pace." Which merits a smug little lip curl as the critical MD reaches over the now screaming Baby N (who's just had a flu shot, don't get me started) and hands over a chart listing dates and "Developmental Event Markers." That's when I realize why I instantly hated the woman. She reminds me of Miss Keebler, the school librarian whose massive calves I had to massage in kindergarten after I accidently bonked them with a stack of Wonder Books I knocked off her desk. The second Cinderella smacked her shinbone, she grabbed my face and told me to get down on my knees and rub her legs. Even then it seemed a little S&My. I can still remember how hot her stockings felt, under her rolled-up donuts, like I was handling two huge, musty bratwursts. Fortunately the incident had no effect, and I grew up perfectly normal, with no kinks whatsoever.

·　·　·

As we're leaving—finally—the superior pediatrician barks that we need to put Bink on her stomach and make her stay there, even if she cries, for ten minutes at a time, with five minute breaks. We try this, when we get home. After ten seconds the baby's whimpering. Around twenty, she's cranking the volume. Before a minute passes, she is wailing as if, to my parentally warped ears, impaled on some laughing Nazi's bayonet at Auschwitz.

Say what? For some reason, kinder-killing Nazis have been on my mind since word of the Newtown slaughter. We hear about it as we're pulling out of the Despero Medical parking lot, across from a bar called Oinkies and a Winnebago outlet. An SS trademark was roaring into some little village, separating parents and kids, then famously tossing babies in the air and catching them on their bayonets before dispatching the victims' older brothers and sisters in front of their horrified (there is no adjective that does the reality justice) parents. A million-and-a-half children were murdered by the Germans. It was national policy. In the same way, as many pointed out after Connecticut, that it's policy to create more dead children via drones in Pakistan, or rockets in Gaza, or to ignore dead children in Chicago. (Media prefer to focus, as Cornel West likes to say, on the "vanilla" victims.) And let's not even get into industries that pour money into Congress to keep regulations lax on childhood-cancer-causing chemicals in food, or GMOs, or air-ruining pollution, or, waiting in the wings, fracking, which pretty much seeds the American earth with human-destroying compounds. (Slower than a bullet but just as effective, killing-wise.)

But hey, enough happy talk. It's Christmas. Or, by the time you're reading this, post-Christmas, and that means time to think about the Son of God. Of course God, Himself, is the original OG Dad. If you believe the Bible, when He had Jesus, the Old Man was already older than time, having (allegedly) invented it. If He exists, I'm guessing that his back is killing Him. And that, if there's CNN on high, He drinks Himself to sleep.

#15: Tot Bites Dog

8 Months Old

S O I'M STANDING IN front of the fridge, door open, wondering more-or-less what happened to my life, when I suddenly remember I have an eight-month-old baby in my arms. I close the door before her face freezes, already picturing the visit from Social Services, me trying to explain why the tip of my daughter's nose is missing— frostbite!—and how one ill-fated fridge loiter does not necessarily make me a bad parent. *I wasn't hungry, I just wanted something, and I didn't know what it was...* I could, but won't, go into how, when I was a child, my own mother, a smart woman partial to long stretches in bed with the curtains closed, would sometimes shout at the ceiling, "I want something and I don't know what it is…"

(Are the voices in our heads congenital? And why does mine sound like Eartha Kitt? So many questions!)

Do you ever just open the refrigerator door and stare? Does that count as meditation?

If I were to keep a fatherhood journal (which I don't, I'm less organized than amoebae), I'd title it *Close Calls*. I mean, for fuck's sake, when it's actually in your arms, how can you forget you have a child? (Full disclosure: when I originally wrote this, I typed, "How can you forget you *are* a child." Jesus. In Typo Veritas.)

Anyway, two nights ago, my girlfriend E and I are sitting there like normal Americans, watching some riveting swill on TV, our newly-tankish little post-half-year-old propped on the couch between us. And, yeah, thanks for asking, we *were* watching *I'd Kill For A Baby* on Discovery Health. (Why an hour of insane ladies stalking and slashing late-term mothers-to-be or snatching newborns out of Walmart parking lots qualifies as "Health" is a question I'll leave for the Discovery execs. They're the professionals. It's like a diet network that shows people killing deli workers, binging on pastrami, and dying. But what do I know?) After pretending to be pregnant to family and coworkers, we're told, and after making home videos of themselves unwrapping baby shower presents, these desperate wanna-moms will stop at nothing to lose the pillows strapped to their guts and get their bloody mitts on an actual infant. Which was not what got me so het up I scared my own child into primal, wailing panic when I banged a fist off the coffee table and nearly doused her with tomato soup. (Miraculously—and happily—it splashed on either side of her, creating the jarring spectacle of a tiny child sitting on a throne of blood, like a Kurosawa warlord.)

No, what made me lose my shit was that AT&T commercial, maybe you've seen it, where some smarmy douche asks a bunch of children whether "bigger is better." A cute little girl spouts some blather that concludes with her saying how she wouldn't want to have a small tree house, and the smarmy guy turns to the little sweetheart and says, "That's a pain in the buns."

"Bigger is better?" *"Pain in the buns?"* In a conversation with schoolchildren? Is it me?

In what pedophilic funhouse was this splash of corporate splooge squeezed out?

Absolutely fucking disgusting, on nine different levels. I imagine some wax-lipped descendent of an actual madman snirkling to himself as he sneaks this one past the client. Until it occurs to me, maybe it wasn't the client. Maybe it was AT&T itself who asked for the *Short Eyes* slant. No doubt to appeal to all the crusty old sex tourists who spend big money on Cambodian child rape vacations. I saw in another doc, on NGC, that Phnom Penh was a prime chickenhawk destination. (And hasn't it been great to see National Geographic abandon its musty, pith helmet legacy for the tabloidy heights of *Taboo*—this week, *Prison Love!*—*Doomsday Preppers, Family Guns,* and late night infomercials for Mohatma Gandhi Leg-waxers? He was a man of peace—and his calves were smooth!) What a swell market for a fine corporation like AT&T to cash in on. Every time Grandpa Kiddie-Diddler calls home to let the folks back in Beaver Falls know how much he's enjoying his golden years, it's a nice ka-ching for shareholders. Jean Genet must be beating off in his grave.)

Overreacting to this perv-fest, I bang my hand on the table, and the aforementioned non-hot, low-sodium Earth Garden organic boxed tomato splashes around—but not, as mentioned, actually *on*—our innocent child. A close call (see first paragraph), but what can I say? Being strung out on heroin is donuts with the pope compared to being strung on baby. They're both twenty-four-seven, alternately euphoric and terrifying commitments. Though late-life Dadhood, I would argue (if anybody wanted to argue) takes significantly more balls. (Or idiocy, depending on how you look at it.)

Admittedly, Junkie versus Dad (as opposed to Junkie Dad, which is a whole other story, but I already wrote that one) presents a less-than-PTA-esque apposition. But fuck the PTA. If I'd made my bones as a devil-may-care female impersonator in Taliban-held Marja, I'd zone back to those halcyon days performing my Afghani Liza—have you ever heard "New York, New York" in Pashto?—and dodging homophobic knife-in-the-teeth zealots. But smackheadism is what I know. Besides which, who needs to compare or contrast?

Now that Tiny N has reached the put-everything-in-her-mouth stage, life's become even more of a nonstop potential Poison Control party. At some point you just give up worrying about that green plastic hippo she picked off the bus seat and jammed in her piehole while you were fishing in a diaper bag for a teething biscuit. (A sentence, I'm not going to lie, I could not have conceived of writing five years ago.) It's not like I can yank the biscuit from her toothless maw and spray Bactine on her gums. To her eternal credit, the difficult-to-ruffle E routinely talks me back from foaming, germaphobic paranoia to something like a reasonably cautionary posture. Meaning, essentially, that instead of freaking out when our Pompadoured eighteen-pounder puts the dog's paw in her mouth, I simply remove it. And try not to obsess on what fecal smorgasbord the adorable, poop-sniffing basenji has pranced through.

To paraphrase that old hippie chestnut, sometimes the bear eats you, sometimes your baby tries to eat the bear.

In truth, now that my fear-free little girl greets the world with mouth open, ready to lick, gum, or swallow anything in sight, I have this recurring image: legions of yawping, grasping infants, tummying their way from shore to shore, shoving everything—rocks, bum-shoes, Audis, Jehovah's Witnesses, and possibly their own parents into their mouths, in some Lilliputian takeover of the world of us shady adults. And, for reasons I myself can't fathom, I find the notion vaguely reassuring.

Of course, I'm writing this at hell fifteen in the morning, scribbling in the dark after Baby N has yowled herself awake. I watch my blue-eyed wailer alternately shlucking her mother's ravaged nipple and raising her still-soft head to peer my way and smile. Making sure, no doubt, to let me know whose fucking world it really is.

#16:
Zero
Dark
Dirty

Diaper

8 Months Old

ELATION THIS MORNING.

I read in *The New York Times* about feces transplants—quite possibly the future of post-antibiotic intestinal medicine—and the future of my entire family suddenly seemed rosy. With the amount of shit my daughter generates in one day, she could put herself through college, or maybe buy a college. The article did not specify how much a pound of healthy tot feces goes for on the black market, but if it's anything like kidneys and livers, I'm sniffing a Bentley in the garage by Christmas. Picture Chiwetel Ejiofor from *Dirty Pretty Things*, only instead of uncovering a hotel organ removal racket, he stumbles on a hospital nursery running an industrial baby crap factory.

You don't consider, going into child rearing, the amount of fecal-centric activity you're going to be enjoying with your child. In my own case, the grumpy business is amplified by the fact that I also walk two dogs in the morning. And, as is custom in my neck of the planet, I stuff a batch of plastic shitbags in my pocket before I leave the house, and pause to gather up dog-bombs as they drop and sneak them into the nearest garbage cans. (In Nick Tosches's wrongly overlooked masterpiece, *In The Hand Of Dante,* the author devotes some serious ink to the grisly phenom of humans picking up canine waste, and is suitably repulsed. For this giant of American literature, the practice embodies, more or less, the Decline of Western Civilization. It's a powerful notion. And I'm with him—though, in all honesty, my concerns at the moment are more mercenary. The potential for bootleg feces, it suddenly hits me, could be huge. With enough dogs in his posse, a guy could make serious money. I could be the Henry Ford of Fido-bagging.)

•   •   •

HOURS LATER, AT THE 10:30 a.m. baby-friendly matinee at our local multiplex—this week, *Zero Dark Thirty*—I find myself watching a man strapped to a wall with his pants at his ankles while my eight-month-old lolls on a blanket on the theater floor, footloose and diaper free. The whole thing feels very Mapplethorpe/Nan Goldin-ish, had Garlic Nan or Mapplethorpe been inclined to feature naked-from-the-waist-down toddler-voyeurs in their shots. Either way, of course, the torture isn't real—it's just, you know, entertainment. But still… The images are big, blaring, and on-screen, and I can't help but ponder the savage wonders no doubt churning, that very moment, in my offspring's nascent psyche. (See Melanie Klein, below.)

Truth be told, I missed the peanut butter on genitalia action—you can only half focus during your Mommy and Me, what with the actual "Me" in question needing semi-constant tending. Still, the juxtaposition of screamy detainee and screamy baby is a not-undisturbing one, especially when the screaming is accompanied by manic, under-one-year-old giggle-howls. The random babies in these M&Ms have a way of communicating, below (or beyond) language, and it is hard not to read meaning into their collective *wahs* and *dah-dahs* during the "enhanced interrogation" scenes. Hard not to picture pink-cheeked Dick Cheney, on his back and waggling his fat white legs, chittering happily, and tugging his turgid pee-pee as the on-screen pain-fest surges on.

With assorted parents and spawn arrayed on seats and carpet for public diapering, the entire theatre morphs into a kind of poopatorium. But, in truth, our girl didn't just stay naked for her dipe change, she stayed that way for half the movie, cooing delightedly at the breeze in her pudenda, while Jessica Chastain moved relentlessly toward that patriots-will-cream-in-their-popcorn boffo ending, locating and smoking the villainous bad actor-with-a-beard. (The actor in question being Ricky Sekhon, a Brit whose role involved playing dead in a bodybag. With a beard. Step aside, Ian McKellen!)

The Mommy and Me torture fest left N happy as a clamcake, even as it left her parents seriously creeped out. (*Yay! We're America, and we'll make you wear panties, show your junk to white women, and stuff you in a box for twenty-four hours to get you to tell us what we want!*) What little girl doesn't dream of growing up, hanging with the boys, and hanging putative terrorists from meathooks in the ceiling? Will N now eschew My Little Pony for Tiny Taliban, anatomically correct Al Qaeda to suspend from hooks in baby's first black site fun kit? For that matter, will little kids still play army—or will they now play drone, and simply launch firecracker-rigged hot dogs at each other? Too soon to tell. Though—as far as Baby N goes—her fave prelingual toy of the moment is a scruffy tractor that's missing a wheel and painted the color of farm mud. (The great thing about flea market toys, for you parents on a budget, is that they come pre-broken, so you don't have to worry about shelling big bucks only to find pieces of whatever the hell you just bought lodged under the couch with the molting Christmas Huggie and the missing pink bunny hat.)

Driving home, post *ZDT*, when the little bugger looks up with those blue eyes and goes ga-ga just like a movie baby, I wonder if the movie was such a good move. Why not just head to Texas, strap her in her stroller, and roll her to an execution?

I have, as it happens, just been reading Melanie Klein, Godmother of Child Therapists, and her theories of the ultra-aggressive fantasies brewing in the dark hearts of children everywhere. Could taking my gurgly daughter to a Kathleen Bigelow torture porn trigger the inner torments already roiling under her fontanel? (And, by the way, can we talk about the whole notion of this wafer-thin, throbbing soft spot above my baby's brain-pudding, vulnerable to a world of flying pencils, ice picks, and poorly child-proofed table edges? No wonder Klein thought children were borderline mini-psychotics. They basically have a tiny, trauma-susceptible scrotum slice wedged on top of their heads. Who wouldn't be annoyed?)

It's no picnic, being a prelingual ankle-biter. But thanks to a medical breakthrough, and my baby's bounteous output, her future may be paved with diapers of gold.

#17:
Thes
Thin
Hapı

e
gs
pen
8 Months Old

"**I** THINK I ACCIDENTALLY tea-bagged my twins… Seriously, we were about to take a bath together. The kids were already in the tub. I was just, you know, lowering myself in the tub when my wife walked into the bathroom to give me shit about something and I just kind of stopped, in sort of a half squat, and before I knew it I felt these tiny little heads, like two little croquet balls, against my underscrote. I was afraid to look down, Felicia says I got Franny right on the forehead, and Jake kind of on top. Right on the soft spot…"

The snippet above was recorded verbatim, from a man I'll call "Kenny" at a New Dad Support Group I attended. It is, of course, wrong on too many levels to contemplate. But what truly disturbs, as much as the mechanics of the incident itself—up to and including use of the term "underscrote," which I've never heard before and, truth be told, could live without hearing again—was the grotesque reference to his child's fontanel.

Another fellow, whose name I knew only as Ted from Altadena, seemed to share my revulsion. "Whoa, dude, slow down! That's not technically a teabag. There was no intent. But still, man… I mean, you really did kind of Tetleyed your son's soft spot?" We were in a back booth at Denny's. Five New Dads, of every socio-economic stripe. Ted looks at me, conspiratorially, and shrugs. "You ask me," he whimpers, wiping his palms on his pant legs, as if to smear off the psychic quease, "the whole thing feels like some kind of gypsy curse…"

Even now, transcribing the chunk of New Dad convo from my notebook to my computer, I feel like drilling a hole in my skull and pumping Purell inside. I guess the moral is—it's not easy being a New Dad. (That, or stuff cotton in your ears before you attend a support group for nervous pops. I don't know what I expected—maybe tips on getting your baby to drool somewhere besides your chest when you carry them. (The white stains, inevitably in nip range, make it look like *I'm* the one who's lactating.) Or ways to keep from scooping your eyes out with a serrated grapefruit spoon and sinking them in mulch after watching your eigtheenth consecutive pre-dawn rerun of *The Chica Show*. On the Sprout Network—which is where we get *Sesame Street* in my neck of the DIRECTV parental woods. (I'm not, by the way, one of those people who thinks TV is bad for children and you should never let a youngster near one. I mean, I was, once upon a time, but then I actually had a kid and had to deal with the yawning hours of non-sleep screaming and crying and couldn't bear to read another Golden book or play another five minutes with the talking doggy. It knows my child's name, and keeps asking her if she's happy, and since I don't know to turn it off I finally had to dismember it.)

•   •   •

ANYWAY, HOW I ENDED up at the New Dad meeting was, I met a guy at a zoo party. You do things like this, go to zoo parties, when you have a baby. The zoo party was a birthday event a musician friend of mine was having for his three-year-old. Which is how I came to hear the spectacularly unsavory, if wholly believable, paternal creep-fest shared by this poor shlub cited above.

"Boundary issues," was Ted from Altadena's ultimate explanation for the lamentable soft spot incident. Strange territory, fatherhood. Occasionally deeply creepy. I didn't go back to the New Dad confabs. Mostly because I didn't need to hear anybody else's parental agita. (Least of all involving involuntary bathtub twin tea baggage.)

Meanwhile, my own child has been whining nonstop for days, coughing like a sixty-year-old with a quart of Four Roses and a three-pack-a-day Chesterfield habit. Worse, I know where she got sick. In fact, I can precisely identify the time and place. Three Saturdays ago, at 6:15 p.m., in the ER of the Hollywood Presbyterian Hospital. Waiting room. We'd gone there, by way of adventure, when E stuck her finger in a portable blender. Long story. Short version, we earned ourselves a four-hour slot in the pain lottery, with all the other walk-in fevers, bleeding eyeballs, stricken grandparents, tweaky hipsters, and chattering, scab-faced schizophrenics likely to slog in out of the dark on any Hollywood Saturday night for a little ER Time.

What made it worse—beyond my girlfriend's anguish at seeing her left forefinger newly morphed into tomato paste—was that we had, by necessity, to bring our eight-month-old into this inferno. Even that would not have been so bad, had not a curious cultural phenomenon kicked in within five minutes of our arrival. Namely, the propensity for old Russian ladies to squeeze her cheeks, grab her feet, and generally manhandle our child. Every time one of these Gromyko-faced babushkas paddled by, I'd find myself testy as Mr. Whipple screaming "Don't squeeze the Charmin" at grabby customers. If I fend one off on the left, another bubkas up behind me and rubs noses. Mostly a stoic decorum reigns among the ER denizens. But our blue-eyed baby exerts some kind of pull on these aggressively grandmotherly émigrés. Before I could intervene, one lady, with a face remarkably like Christopher Lee in the 1966 Hammer Films classic, *Rasputin the Mad Monk* (if Christopher Lee had put on about eighty-nine pounds, all in the face) was literally coughing into a sopping hanky with one hand and pinching Bink's cheeks with the other. No sooner had I shooed her away than a second, more Khrushchev-esque intruder sidled up.

There seemed no way to stop the former Soviet bloc putsch. "Is Russian baby!" each babushka announced. Before proceeding to douse her with Borscht-resistant cold germs that had her coughing up hamhock-sized Cracker Jack prizes for the next month.

Of course, there is the theory that the more germs the baby's exposed to, the greater resistance your baby will have. Dousing her in the detritus of a Saturday night Hollywood ER, our child may well have an Armor All immunity for the foreseeable future. That or she'll come down with Moscow fever and we'll have to nurse her back to life with blini. At which point she will also emerge stronger and better equipped for a tough, toxic tomorrow. As a viral astronaut for the former Soviet Union.

Still, all I can think about is the accidental family tea-bagger. "Hey," was the last thing Kenny the Bathtub Miscreant pleaded, "accidents happen."

Sad, but true. I'm accidentally never going back to my New Dad Support Group. But not because of the disturbo and disgraced priestly over-share. (I've heard stranger—there was another fellow who could not bring himself to hug his one-year-old because she had eyes just like his mother, who used to make him do the mashed potatoes in monkey pajamas for her lady's bridge group, which he claims is the source of his lifelong performance anxiety with women.)

Sometimes I think they should require psychological profiles, or at least learner's permits, for parenthood. But then, how many of us would be here if they did?

#18:
When
Good
Go Ba

Babies
9 Months Old

M Y DAUGHTER GOT HER first bill today. Twenty-five dollars, a cancellation fee for blowing off an appointment with a Dr. Papoolian. A woman who, the first time we saw her, decried our child for not being up to all her milestones. She should be pulling herself up on the bars of her crib. She should be singing. She should be crawling. She should be doing Sudoku.

That was eight weeks ago. By now she's climbing. And singing—or maybe, more accurately, scatting, since she doesn't actually know any words yet besides "dada," "ha-mmm," and something that sounds suspiciously like "dork," which she only busts out when she's staring at me and pointing. (How could she know?) What she doesn't do is crawl. At least, not forward. Mysteriously, she can—when flat on her back, and possessed of the urge—do a kind of dry-land backstroke, kicking her little sausage-rockets and launching herself in the opposite direction of where she actually wants to go. It shows on her face—the alternate consternation at going the wrong way, and the sheer delight of going anywhere.

But still—baby's first bill! "Today you are an American!" I tell her. "You owe money. If you don't pay it, they'll send more bills. If you don't pay it for long enough, they'll actually come after you. And," I admit, "I was looking forward to the moment when we get a call, pick it up, and it's the collection agency demanding to know if N can come to the phone." Maybe they'll send somebody around to repo her Jumperoo.

It's all got me stirred up. Sleepless. Which works out well, since tonight my child is sleepless, and I actually have an excuse for sitting in the dark and staring at the TV at three-forty-blow-my-brains-out in the morning. And—I can't lie—I'm back to binging on Healthy Times vanilla teething biscuits. And, again, I feel sort of Sylvia Plath-y, without the whole head-in-the-oven thing. I mean, I'm not really depressed, I'm just daddy-zombied. And daddy doesn't have it half as bad as mommy, who, lately, must endure hours with baby lodged on chest, jaw locked on her nipple like a bear trap with butt-dimples. Now that our tiny clamper has sprouted teeth, the situation has moved from mild discomfort to flat-out flesh pain. I sometimes wake in the night to see E staring straight ahead in the dark—the whites of her eyes slightly harrowing—N snoring and sleep-chomping atop her.

When Sweet Pea does cease nip-nibbling, it's generally to revolve on her axis, so she can kick one of us in the face. It's Discovery Channel-y, the means by which our twenty-pounder finds the exact position for maximal mom and dad face-kicking. (Shout out to Claude Bessy, aka "Kickboy Face," late founder of *Slash* magazine and Catholic Discipline.) Was this repetitive foot-in-teeth maneuver, like the stock video of mama and baby cheetah tussling on all the big cat shows, preparation for real-life survival face-kicking down the road? Or is it simply that our offspring hates the fact that we have all our teeth, and she doesn't, so she'd really like to heel-smack some of ours out?

Now it's nearly four, and we're watching a *Sesame Street* rerun, so the poignancy of the moment is charged by retro knowledge of Elmo's dismissal due to underage sex charges. Too bad he didn't work for the Pope, or he could have kept his job and just been transferred to another kid's show.

The night was interesting before this. We took N on a baby date. Tots love other tots. And the tot N loves right now is a year-and-changer with a biblical name and Evel Knievel tendencies. Cool kid. I'm crazy about the little guy. And when, in the middle of the meal, I watched him crawl randomly across the floor of a Mexican restaurant, with the fearlessness of a blind man on PCP, I thought I saw my daughter's eyes widen, unbridled fascination spread her lips in a vivid smile. I think the technical term is smitten. "That's how it is," E says, stabbing a ball of guacamole with a corn chip, then crunching it. "Little girls like bad little boys."

I'd never seen a grown stuntman take as many face-plants as N's baby boyfriend. It was impressive. Despite my trepidation that she'd follow in his—well, not footsteps, since neither of them walk; belly-grime, maybe—I had to admit, it was impressive. And I was wondering at what point my little girl would take an itch to make her bones by bellying her way across a four-lane freeway at rush hour.

Perv jacket or not, I found it soothing to just listen to Elmo—in character—and not worry about the future, the big dangerous world, and the smooth-tongued one-year-olds out to lure my pride and joy into potentially fatal restaurant floor-crawls.

It will happen, soon enough. For now, give me *Sesame Street* and teething biscuits. Wild times. We'll pay the bills later.

When good babies go bad.

It happens to all of us. Eventually.

#19:
The
Screa

cm

O MONTHS OLD

I T'S NO SECRET, THE amount of crying you have to listen to when you have a baby is astronomical. Before this, my exposure to crying females was pretty much limited to those I was in a relationship with—along with the odd grieving aunt at funerals (in my family the women were screamers, not weepers), or John Boehner. (Who, for some reason, I think of as a crying female—no offense to females.) Now, however, full-tilt tot-wailing is such a daily part of my aural diet, I'm almost sort of within shouting distance of being able to deal with non-stop infantile shrieks. I won't say I don't notice it, but it's no longer so nerve-peelingly unendurable. Unless of course you're stuck in a car, rendered immobile by inexplicably dense, gluey LA traffic, and the ten-month-old your seed helped spark to life is unleashing an aria of under-one pain squalls, reaming her own lungs as if chained to a radiator in a Rumanian orphanage having her head shaved by beefy, rough-handed matrons who use babies as chow-hall hockey pucks and have no hearts.

E, by now, has mastered the art of pulling over and whipping N's dipe off, scooping poop out, bapy wiping her ass, and slapping a new diaper on faster than a crew pit at NASCAR. Or is it the Indy 500? I was trying to snag a whole new demo with that metaphor, but in reality one of the two race car drivers I could name is Dale Earnhardt Jr., and even that's just because of the band Dale Earnhardt Jr. Jr. (You have to wonder, were there lawsuits involved? Did the original Jr. Dale demand the royalties from "Simple Girl"?) AJ Foyt never had that problem, though he had a cooler name.

The car thing is brutal because there is—literally—nowhere to go. The noise just bounces around in those four little windowed walls. It's like being trapped in a portable season of *American Horror Story: Asylum*, all thirteen episodes compressed into one rolling hell-yowl, without Jessica Lange deranging from seat to seat. Lately E's taken to riding in back of the Caddy, sitting beside little N, in hopes her proximity will dim the impulse to blow out the windshield with a single, piercing, my-parents-are-monsters note. One parent/neighbor with five-month-old twins actually suggested an adult car seat. Before the conversation, I didn't know they had those. I'm still not sure the poor woman, clearly outgunned by a pair of chew-crazy under-oners, is telling the truth, or if she's delusional. It happens. I haven't taken the time to Google "adult carseats" (who has the energy?) but if they actually do have them, and they'd help put a damper on our daughter's ear-bleeding screams we'd both hop in and buckle our crotch buckles. (Future headache for child: dad's got a Prius and a ten-year-old Cadillac, which makes him automotively revolting at both the Elvis and the Ed Begley Jr. poles of existence.)

All of the above, by the way, was written with a yowling child—my yowling child—in her crib five feet away. She's not just screaming, she's eyeballing me, giving me the pre-crawler mad dog treatment as she blasts bloody nodes off her factory-fresh voicebox. Has anyone done studies on the effect of nonstop eye contact infant screeching? Are there PhDs on the subject? Did doctoral candidates with young children perhaps decide to focus on their own spawn and end up standing in front of the mirror playing with their own hair for hours on end and muttering, "Mommy sad," instead?

Of course, implicit—unspoken?—in this OGD's reaction to baby screaming is the simple fact that baby gets to scream, while daddy doesn't. Babies can scream whenever they want. They can also unburden their bowels and touch themselves in public with impunity. I'm not claiming these questionable privileges inspire jealousy—I mean, either one of those would be creepy for a man over fifty, right? I am simply saying, forget the random crapping and crotchy touches, I would fucking love to wail at the top of my lungs when life didn't go my way. Who wouldn't? I don't even need a reason. Just once, I would like to curl up on the floor of a supermarket, perhaps in the housewares aisle, and unleash my inexplicable, keening grief, just howl like an endangered timber wolf with his paw caught in an trap somewhere outside Nome. (Or is it Gnome? I give up.)

Babies are like the sidewalk screamers who used to rule New York when I lived there in the seventies. Back then, babbling and screaming out loud on the street still got you looks. (This was before cell phones.) Now, what makes life even more worth living is walking into a store or restaurant with a high-decibel wriggler in your arms. It's not just the accusatory head-turning—I get that anyway, from just being a dick my age with a cool, young girlfriend and a tot in tow—it's the impossible-to-avoid thought-balloons above each head, the ones that say: "What have you done to that poor child?"; "What kind of twist-case are you?"; or "Wait until I call Social Services!"

What unifies them all is a level of self-righteous, hateful, and bilious viciousness which—until I lately fathered a Diaper Diva—I saw only once before, in the face of a grandmother in a black-and-white photo spitting on the corpse of Mussolini, hanging upside-down in a Milan Esso Station. I think the term I'm looking for is war criminal. Or the parental equivalent thereof. The implication being that if a creature is wailing so loudly, so relentlessly, with such absolute, soul-searing, desperate ferocity, then there has to be a reason. Though, as anyone who's been around one can tell you, babies don't have to have reasons. In that respect, they're a lot like us. The difference being that it's appropriate for babies to behave like babies. We don't get to scream. Except on the inside. Like I'm doing right now. Like, I cringe to admit, I probably do for about a quarter of any given day. (Am I being wildly optimistic?) Until young N, who has just learned to wave—a dainty palm-and-finger waggle accompanied by a coy smile into her own shoulder—decides to cease roiling and wave at me. And then, of course, it's like the screaming never happened. Like my heart and eardrums aren't shattered in fifteen different places. And all is well in the world.

I've died and been cuted back to life.

I mean, how can you not love the little fuckers?

#20:
One
Birth
Editi

Year
day
on

ONE YEAR OLD

"IT'S PARTY TIME! TIME to party like a big girl!" That's Dora talking. Dora the Explorer. You may have seen her show. I hadn't, before I received the Dora doll in the mail, anonymously. (Which we'll get to.)

It took me a few listens to realize what Dora was saying was potty, not party. This was the Dora the Explorer potty doll. "I know that I can do it!" she sings, when you press the button in (of all places) her left butt cheek. "So come on, let's get to it!" Trickle-trickle. Then, "Mommy…I did it. I went to the potty!" Followed by—*whoosh*!

That whoosh is actually more of a flushing thing, after which comes the proud imprecation:"Vamos a lavarnos las manos!" *Let's wash our hands*, in Spanish.

Of course, the gift wasn't intended for me. It was for my daughter, on her first birthday. The Big Oh-One. But there was no card, and Dora's mug looks alarmingly like Cha-Cha, a Peruvian ex-sex worker with whom I'd spent a fairly heinous, if eventful, three weeks in my twenties. Cha-Cha owned a luxury condo in Iquitos. Financed by dressing like a Catholic schoolgirl and peeing her panties for big time narcotraficantes and hedge fund managers who'd spank her and call her a "dirty little angel." My last vision of her was wielding a kebab spear at my exposed testicle behind a Lima bowling alley. Surprisingly, it didn't end well. Just thinking this, while simultaneously playing with my child, stands out as an epic Daddy Shame moment. (I don't know how it is for other guys, but there are chunks of my past so foul and inconsistent with my current Elder Dad status that just letting them in my head, as I dawdle my little love bug, is like screaming, "I suck Satan's Cock" at a PTA meeting.)

Dora comes with her own little potty. (Which, weirdly, looks more like a bucket.) But you don't have to know Cha-Cha to know there's something pervy about the whole thing. "Can you imagine the guy who designs these?"

E says. It's kind of hard not to. "I wonder how many registered sex offenders violate parole when their PO finds Dora the Dripper in their sock drawer." (Breastfeeding while making this observation). But Baby N loves it, and we spend the day watching her dance along while Dora warbles about what a potty girl she is.

Anyway, it's a big day. A year! A birthday party! Other parents at my house—which, while (I'm not going to lie) initially terrifying, is—comparatively—great. It's when you're at somebody else's kiddie party, and you're trapped over a wading pool with a Hipster Insurance Salesman Dad who wants to sell you a "rockin' homeowner's policy" that things can get, what's the word, *unfuckingbearable*? (How long, exactly, can selling insurance be ironic?) If Insurance Salesman dad had an ex-girlfriend-sending-voodoo-piss-doll policy, then I might sign up. Otherwise, I just had to breathe cilantro breath while my daughter and his son sat in the mud giggling and poking each other in the stomach. It looked like a lot more fun.

As he got drunker, hipster Insurance Dad downshifted into overshare. Father had a heart attack while watching kiddie porn. The police said if he lived they'd have to arrest him. So we all sat around hoping he would die. At this, I excused myself to change a diaper. Any diaper. It didn't even have to be a baby's. I just wanted to get out of there. (People tell me things, what can I say? When you write a memoir including boatloads of your own atrocities, folks just feel comfy sharing theirs.)

This being a birthday situation, parental conversation turns, inevitably, to milestones and percentiles. As in: "My Arthur's nine months. He's in the fifth percentile for head size and the ninety-fifth for body mass. I'm a little concerned." Percentiles are fixed, but milestones are competitive. And by milestone I mean things that your child does before any other child. Eye contact is an early milestone, later big ones are talking, crawling, walking, and suing.

At the same birthday fête where I met Insurance Daddy, there was a little Saltine of a man, a lawyer, who wanted me to know "we were 'f-ing' blown away when Jebediah started crawling at four months. By five, he started walking." At half a year, apparently, the tyke was doing highlights from *Riverdance*. I'd never actually met anyone who said "f-ing" before. What **is** that? Is he afraid to say, "fuck?" Does he think he's on *Fresh Air?* Whatever, I didn't mention it. For that matter, I did not mention that my own child, at eleven months, had just started to pull herself on table edges and stand. (Unlike Jeb, the hipster-biblical little shit.) Standing on her own was still a bridge too far. And walking—what's walking?

Why didn't I mention this to Jebediah's proud pop? Because I'd learned my lesson, that's why. Three weeks ago, I made the mistake of confiding to another newish pop I'd just met that my daughter had just commenced crawling. (In a kind of hip-slung, leg-draggy manner my older daughter—one of the funniest people I know—describes as "like the girl in *The Exorcist* scuttling down the stairs.")

After I shared my crawl stats, Milestone Dad stepped back in horror. "Dude, does the baby's mom do opiates? That shit gets in the breast milk." Said with a mask of concern that barely covered his gloating. "No," I said, "it's not her thing." "What about alcohol? Babies can get loaded if a woman drinks, like one glass of wine and gives milk. Dude, seriously."

Dig it. I've known the guy three minutes, and he's already attributing my daughter's mobility schedule to…maternal degeneracy. Shared parenthood gives him the right! We're all experts! For what must be the thousandth time, I commend myself on the uplifting effect late inning Dadhood has had on my soul. I can no longer contemplate homicide without thinking of my child growing up without a father. So I don't strangle the dude-guy. I don't even poke an eye out. That's growth!

Nobody ever brings up "milestones" unless their little Honey or Heinrich measures up in the top ten. I have my own theory: that early milestone babies are like the people who were popular in high school. They end up working at the DMV—if McDonalds isn't hiring. Instead of telling him his kid will end up in a Mickey D suit, I dusted off my Einstein anecdote. How young Albert did not talk until he was five. People thought he was retarded.

I confess I made up the retarded part. (I know, but this was before people were "mentally challenged," though people should probably be retro-correct.) In any event, I have heard though, for a fact, that the father of relativity was a late talker and tardy to master shoelaces. Look it up.

But fuck me. I began this anniversary edition wanting to charm and delight with the fun-wonders of a baby turning one. Instead I'm compelled to talk about screaming. Again.

See, after parties, our little one can get over-stimulated. Wail-y. Driving with a tantrum-tot is like having a car fight with someone willing to scream fifty times louder than you, nonstop. On the other hand, babies don't jump out of the vehicle while it's moving, as most of the grown women I've been involved with were wont to do. So there's that.

Pre-one, Little N did her share of crying. As babies do. But post-one she's become inconsolable. Operatic. Confirming E's theory of babydom. All babies are drama queens. There's fist waggling, head shaking, a pained, stricken look on that tiny face bespeaking a level of betrayal for which there are no words. (Just as well. Since the only words she knows are "dada," "mama," "good doggy," and something that sounds oddly like "stank.")

Rule of thumb, for newcomers: rate of volume increase in baby screaming is inversely proportional to the energy spent trying to make a baby stop screaming. In this sense, screaming babies exist as metaphors for the universe. Diapered humility machines.

What can I say? At one, my daughter owns an other-worldly cuteness I can only compare to Humphrey Bogart in his Gerber Baby days.

I have, I confess, come to discriminate baby-types: there are the little professors, the lumps, the boys-who-are-already-dicks, the flirty nine-monthers (girls or boys.) And then there's Baby N—the pass-her-around-an-old-age-home-to-cheer-up-nonagenarians type. N's got a smile, but it's not all over the place. That reluctance to give it up makes people melt into puddles when she goes into some kind of smile storm and starts throwing them around. Plus she wears her hair in a vertical sprout atop her head, like Pebbles. Don't get me started…

The one avoid-at-all-costs of a column like this is the "cute thing my baby does" anecdote. One wrong move and you're a Japanese YouTube laughing fat baby video. Which, don't get me wrong, is great for when you're fucking around in the office. (Or, so I assume. It's been decades since I've had a job involving an office.)

Of course we could make our own videos, but I'm not sure they'd be—what's the word?—appropriate. Because babies just aren't appropriate. At least mine isn't. Even E is creeped out when, in the course of suckling, our daughter reaches over and starts stroking mommy's other tit, complete with Barry White slaps and nipple tweaks, like she's trying to change the dial on a clock radio. It happens.

(As I write this, mind you, Baby N is pressing and repressing Dora's button. "Potty like a big girl!" Whoosh!)

But never mind. Right now it's time for some Parenting Theory. I think after a year I have earned the right to pontificate. In brief, for you note-takers, there are two kinds of parents: (1) The kind who tells their children how wonderful life is, and all the wonderful things there are to enjoy within it; and, (2) those who tell their babes how dangerous life is, and can't help listing all the things that can kill them. Let's call them the Joyheads versus Feargivers.

For example: watching N scoot across the living room floor in her diaper, E delights in our baby's newfound freedom. "Look," she coos, on her knees in front of the baby, "Bink can go anywhere. She's a world traveller."

(I should say that seeing a woman on her knees in front of you, with her ass in the air, means one thing before you have a baby, a whole other when the reason she's on the floor is because you mated a while ago, and now you're chasing a toddler around. See what happens!)

At one point we did find ourselves saying fuck it, let's fuck, while our gurgly issue had her face buried in an upside down Dr. Seuss

book across the room. It was all systems go
for a few minutes. Then Little N took her nose
out of *Hop On Pop* and started shrieking, at
which point we had to make the decision, do
we finish or do we grab the screaming baby?
This is about character, my friends. So basically
I finished, and then we stopped. I mean, that's
how it is with a kid; sacrifices must be made.
There will be other opportunities. We just
have to learn to take the odd pleasure with a
wailing accompaniment. (And not, Freud aside,
obsess on what a baby might remember from
its preverbal years, decades later. To live, in the
best of times, is to be vaguely traumatized.)

Mysteriously, at the first instance of sexual
contact on the premises, our baby will bolt
upright out of deep sleep and begin to howl.
Apparently she doesn't want a sibling.

But where were we? The two strains of
parent, right. Joy versus Fear. Fun versus Dread.
Kitties are cute! Kitties will scratch your eyes
out! You get the point. My partner, god love
her, watches our newly capable crawler with
unalloyed delight. Me—the nego-parent—slides
straight to the myriad ways she'll now be able to
break her neck, and possibly end up a paraplegic.
The same divergence applies to all endeavors.

(Forgive me. I've been watching *Deadwood* reruns. It makes your writing florid.) Say Baby N and mom are watching *Yo Gabba Gabba!,* the surreal alterna-*Sesame Street,* dancing their little dance moves to Questlove and digging Devo genius Mark Mothersbaugh drawing doggies. Me—much as I love seeing my baby girl getting a taste of art and music—what I'm really doing is stressing over the brain-cancery radiation emitted by the TV. In front of which we spend hours reading books and playing on a rug. (The death rays, I gather, continue unabated whether the big screen's on or off.)

I'm not going to lie. It's hard to be in the now, as Ram Dass used to say, when half of you, at every moment, is obsessing on the cell-mutating power of appliances, electromagnetic waves, and smart phones. It's like the whole world is designed to fuck up my child.

That said, I don't like to think of myself as neurotic. I prefer informed. And I am no germaphobe. I'm of the Michael Pollan, babies-need-to-get-dirty-and-get-colonized-by-bacteria school. Two days ago, not to brag, we hunkered *en famille* in a rabbit hutch inch-deep with bunny turds and rotten cantaloupe husks. And I was fine with it. No problem. But, two hours later, we're in a restaurant, and I'm dying. Why? Because E and Squirmy are giggling and gobbling raspberries—while I'm fixated on the pesticides sprayed on the berries, and the, no doubt, DNA-mutating, genetically modified, Monsanto soybeans in the soymilk we're drinking.

Is the pattern clear? I was raised by a woman who thought going without socks could result in gangrene—because FDR had a grandnephew who once went sockless and lost his leg up to the femur. At three, resting my rat-faced little gaze on the world, I'd already absorbed the lesson: everything fun can kill you. And everything else is dangerous. Life was more chutes than ladders.

By sheer coincidence, my own mother died at about the same time her new grandchild was born. And there's no denying that Grandma's Universe of Menace mentality lives on in Elder-Daddy me. But still...I now realize, on a level I couldn't grasp my first time around the daddy track, that non-stop catastrophizing marks its own kind of love. Maybe destructive, mutant, difficult love, but love all the same. That's how it is for we Eastern-European Semite types. To love is to worry about the bad things that can befall the beloved. (Consider the Holocaust.) We're nervous when the sky is too blue.

I admit, it sounds bleak. On the other hand, I'm wearing a party hat.

Happy birthday, baby. Potty like a big girl.

#21
In the
Interes
Rectal S

of
ecurity
2 YEARS OLD

THE GREAT THING ABOUT having a two-year-old in the house is you feel your mortality like a happy little gun to your head. They're not just growing—*you're dying!*

Does that make sense? Since I was already post middle-aged when my newest daughter dropped in, it felt, in some existential way, like we were crawling past other in different directions. She was new-born, I was newly old.

See, the first time I was a father, I was dying cause I was shooting dope every day. The Big Nod, not to get all queasy-romantic about it, was never more than a syringe plunge away. Now—the good news!—I'm not closing in on death because there's Mexican tar in my arm, it's happening on the natch. You know, the cycle of life.

Why mention this? Because! That's where my Old Guy brain goes of a morning. I have an hour or two around dawn to write before baby and mother wake up. In these hours, the mind travels. I remember what it was like to live alone, and have days to sprawl out and make lots of time for wrestling a few thousand words to the ground. Not writing can eat up a lot of time. But now I'm a workadaddy, to lift a Tom Wolfe-ism, with an honest to god job every day—the first since my late thirties when I wore the proud McDonalds red and gray. Before heading into *Maron* to hang with the other yuck-hucksters, I put in some early AM time honing my long game.

What I like to do is stagger upstairs, after banging out a page or two, and cut up some 'nanas and strawberries for Tot-Girl, just so I can experience the fun of having her look at the fruit, then look at me, then look back at the fruit, then take a tentative nibble and say, "Nico's fine. Nico doesn't need any fruit." Which, aside from sounding like Yankees demigod Reggie Jackson, who used to answer reporters questions with, "That's not good for Reggie," is better than her previous baby move: grabbing the plate and hurling it at the floor for the dogs to scarf up and then shit out later on their favorite rugs.

One of our dogs, the basenji, likes to leave discreet, efficient little turds in out-of-the-way places, so we don't find them for months; by which point they've calcified into tiny turd rocks, generally discovered by N when she's groping for marbles behind a couch. It's disgusting, but on the plus side said basenji has let little N stroke and pummel him and pull his curly tail since she was old enough to maul. When you weigh that against the odd calcified crap nugget, it seems like a square deal.

But I'm not sure. Besides my fear of baby brain cancer (Google bedside cell phones and baby brains), I have an unhealthy obsession with my daughter breathing poop fumes. Because we are on a septic system, and I have consistently forgotten to dump the monthly enzymes in our toilets, I'm also convinced some kind of cell-curdling swamp gas leaks from our commodes. Though so far I'm the only one who can smell it. As my mother used to say, "it's probably your upper lip."

Now that our daughter is toilet trained (except for some random bed-wetting, which I like to think of a tot-homage to Sarah Silverman) I look back on the first two years of her life as a sea of ungodly diaper loads. Once, in a pinch, I changed her on the hood of my old Cadillac, just off a skeevy stretch of Sunset Boulevard, and caught some pervaloid homeless guy smacking his gums and peeping from behind a dumpster. Then he called my name and I realized I'd been to rehab with him. He was my drug counselor. Life.

· · ·

ANYWAY, NOW THAT SHE'S housebroken, our little girl climbs onto the potty all by herself. New to the whole process, she's still in the Kabuki-wiping phase. By which I mean she will bunch up some toilet paper and kind of air-wipe her tushy after going pee-pee. Which is fine, as long as I take a follow-up swipe. Poop involves a bit more choreography, but we're getting there. (And can I mention the cottage industry in poop and potty-centric children's literature. *Once Upon A Potty, A Potty For Me! P Is For Potty!* And the old standby, *Elmo's Potty Time Play-a-Song Book.* The idea, I think, is to turn every bowel movement into a little musical.)

Our goal is to get through the whole toilet transition without shaming her. My own upbringing was a little different. I pretty much left the womb and went straight into a shame spiral. And the seat of all shame, no pun intended, was the toilet itself.

My mother, and I say this with love, was the Herman Goering of anal cleanliness. She was so obsessed with keeping my tiny hinie clean she'd flip out at so much as a chocolate smooch in my underwear. Her threat, of which I've written elsewhere, was that she'd hang my dirty undies on the line in the backyard, "for all your friends to see." My solution, Dr. Freud, was to not move my bowels for weeks at a time. Until Mom whipped out Mister Squeezems, her trusty enema. It was like being raped by Harpo's bicycle horn. The mere sight of which would cause my little boy butt-cheeks to pucker in premonitory dread. To no effect.

Fracking for poop, Mom would inject hot soapy water up my three-year-old ass with a force and conviction that would make Dick Cheney weep. With joy. When I read excerpts from the CIA Torture Report, I could not help picture my late mother at some black site, her stiff Lucille Ball flip intact as she sphinc-slammed some sleep-deprived Yemeni goat-herder into submission.

Could that be the silver lining of enhanced interrogation? Instead of shaming and abusing their own innocent children, our stalwart intelligence agents were shaming and abusing captive Muslims.

Sometimes it's the little things.

I feel safer already.

#22
Kidd
Calm

e

2 YEARS OLD

DAYS WHEN MY DAUGHTER hates me, I console myself that this may be a sign of her discerning nature. Two seconds out of sleep at 8:00 in the morning, she will open her eyes, see my salt-and-pepper craggy-ass grill looming over her and scream, *"Noooo!"*

The sheer adrenal rage in her eyes rocks me back on my heels. And, this is not going to make me look great, but no matter how often it happens, no matter how often her mother reminds me of the obvious ("For fuck sake, she's two!'), it stings a little.

Instantly abject, I blurt reflexively, "Come on, I love you, Picklehead! What are you mad about?"

"Don't say that!" Besides "No," "Don't say that!" is her favorite thing to scream. An endearing stab of censorship and control in a chaotic world, generally followed by ritual floor-flinging. Hands jammed over her eyes, she will freeze into a little anger coma. (Maybe it suddenly occurs to me, she just hates the name "Picklehead.") After which, when I go in for a tickle (mistake) she rolls over onto her back and kicks me in the teeth so hard it uproots the titanium screw I just had stuck in my jaw, to hold an implant. Why the tooth fell out in the first place, who knows? The only certainty is that without it, regardless of alleged IQ, I radiate all the class and gravitas of gap-toothed Monongahela Jew-billy.

Maybe not white trash. White *traife...* separate issue.

Fast forward, it's hours after my morning tot attack, and I'm at a local health food emporium, idly scoping the shelves for some alpha lipoic acid. (Don't ask me what it does, but I know it's spectacular for you. That and turmeric). I'm thinking about this spate of random baby wrath; how, the way I'm wired, if somebody yowls at me, if they hate me, I kind of agree with them; like, if I dig deep enough, I can retro-manufacture a reason for what would otherwise be some inexplicable personal attack. (Call me an asshole and I'll kind of agree, even if I've been nothing but Mother Theresa to you.) It's something my mother helped me with.

What you always wonder with an acting-out tot—what *I* at least, can't help but wonder, is whether or not the current, ah, difficulty, might be permanent. I had a friend whose little girl was a biter. Sweet as could be except when she got pissed off and started chewing holes through classmates faces. After a couple years of attending school with a minder, followed by an effective drug regimen, she's now a sweet, smart tenderhearted teen, whose parents no longer have to worry about her smashing Dr. Seuss books on her baby brother's head. Amazing, how firm and resilient a baby skull is. I have seen Baby N take some bonks on the melon that would dent a Hummer.

But I'm tired, I'm losing the thread. I was going to segue from troubling, there-I-said-it hurtful misbehavior of my own little two-year-old to where I'm currently standing, in the Whole Foods Kiddie aisle. Before me, in colorful packaging, is an array of mood-altering kiddie formulas. Would I be better off grabbing

Siddabrand "Kids 2+" or (my fave) "Temper Tamers," for "Irritability, Short Temper and Tantrums." The product, if I may continue "temporarily relieves symptoms of irritability, short temper, tantrums," plus the ever— troubling "mischievous [sic] and destructive, frustrated and discontented."

And this, friends and working parents, is only one brand. I have not yet mentioned Hylands 4Kids "Calm 'n' Restful." Or Planetary Herbals "Calm Child" or Nerve Support's "Valerian Super Calm." Bioray's got gluten free, dairy, and soy free Calm.

This, mind you, is Los Feliz, Los Angeles, a neighborhood so enlightened half the parents would rather face a firing squad of meat bullets than feed their child gluten. My own folks, back when color TV was new, would occasionally drip a little booze into my milk bottle. Thereby quelling my own toddler torments. And I turned out fine. The idea of feeding valium-and-gin to baby Cooper or ironically named Mabel would, understandably, be anathema to the average Whole Foods Shopper. But slipping baby a homeopathic Roofie, why not? Sometimes even we Vegpas (Vegan parents) need a little—*stop that fucking screaming*—peace.

I'm not judging. I'm identifying.

Though we are, at this writing, the height of the Cosby rape opera, and it's hard not to make the creepy leap from herbal toddler-dosing—so they'll shut up and sleep—to the patented Cosby Compliance Formula. Horrible thought. (And how comes nobody mentions the doctor who wrote prescriptions for all that shit? And, from the doctor's point of view, was knowledge that he was Cosby's go-to rape-meds man good for business or bad? It's certainly a troubling world we bring our children into.)

But fuck that. My titanium screw still hurts. And it's probably crooked now, so my new tooth will be facing outward, at forty-five degrees, giving me a mono-fang, on the left, in the manner of a dentally-challenged vampire. (How come you never see those?) But at the moment, my daughter is sitting on my lap, sucking on a bottle of almond milk, bliss-diddling her bellybutton. We're watching *A Turtles Tale,* which has a cooler soundtrack than *Frozen*. It's been a hug-fest for hours. Tomorrow, there will probably be some wake-up hate. But right now, it all feels right.

That Kiddie Calm really works.

#23
The
Twos

2 YEARS OLD

THERE IS A TRUTH about hanging with babies that nobody talks about. It can be fucking boring. Mind-crushingly, soul-poisoningly boring. But you don't admit it because, you know, parenting is a sacred thing. Even if, no way around it, some days you just kind of find yourself sitting there, toddler on lap, feeling your brain run to slush while you watch the 53,000th episode of *Peter Rabbit*.

It's "The Greedy Fox" episode, where Mr. Tod, the vulpine pedophile, is yet again wanting to scoop up bunny children and put them in his pot. Mr. Tod is now trying to lure Cottontail, Peter's little sister, back to his cottage. And Mr.

Tod fancies skintight tan breeches with a purple plush waistcoat and over-ripe ascot, and is given to squealing in an effeminate manner when stressed. The dandy fox emits a low, pervy growl when he's about to pounce. (As who doesn't?)

I wonder about the people who write these things. I wonder about those days in the writer's room, swilling coffee and cooking up plots for the pedophilic fox and the weirdly Jewy frog, Jeremy Fisher, who spends his days in a tight little three-piece suit, trying to write "the most magnificent symphony in the history of the world. "Imagine a froggy, liver-lipped little Oscar Levant. Minus the pills and cigarettes. Unlike the fey fox, Jeremy Fisher does not want to molest and devour the children. He only wants them to help him make strange sounds.

Clearly, I've given the subject too much thought. But what else is there to do but obsess, speculate, and just kind of…endure. It's horrible to say. But just because the bond between parent and child is sacred, that doesn't mean you do not want to set your face on fire and run in front of a FedEx truck while you and your little one are reading *Sesame Street Hide & Seek,* looking for scorpions on the pyramid. The same scorpions that were there yesterday, and five months ago.

And that we're looking for again right now—while simultaneously watching TV and eating, thereby endowing my little one with the life skills that got me through a rocky middle age, but may not be the best thing on the menu for a two-year-old.

Mind you, after I dumped my BlackBerry—possibly the last man on earth to do so—and could surreptitiously suck up entire backlit novels while watching these *Peter Rabbit* reruns, something else happened. (Peter, by the way, spends his days stealing vegetables from a farmer; carrot-thieving, apparently, being another life skill worth cultivating. Separate issue.) Post iPhone 6, I stumbled into another crisis. Because, as mentioned ad nauseum, I'm one of those people who worry about the death rays emanating from my total convenience device, I'm convinced that my rereading *Naked Lunch* on a glowing screen next to my child's tender head is going to give her cranial blastoma, or some other heinous malignancy. Maybe it's just Burroughs. But I actually feel a little Mengelish exposing her to these possible side effects. I can't help thinking—perseverating—that I'm microwaving her. As if, tip of the hell-hat to the Butcher of Auschwitz, I actually were putting her in an oven. In this case, literally cooking her skull, heating soft tissue inside her beautiful baby dome—thanks (according to Wikipedia, my source in all things life and death) to the rotations of polar molecules induced by the electromagnetic field. Brown and serve.

But, did I say brain? Brain's part of it. But not all. Let me quote: "The brain's blood circulation is capable of disposing of excess heat by increasing local blood flow. However, the cornea of the eye does not have this temperature regulation mechanism temperature regulation mechanism, and exposure of two to three hours duration has been reported to produce cataracts in rabbits' eyes."

Cancer and cataracts. Thanks Dad! (Note to self: do not jam training spoon into temple. It won't help)

My obsession with cell-phone cancer, I can't lie, has blown up beyond all tolerable level. My wife, who sometimes hangs with our lil girl until she falls asleep, has had to bear my hectoring whenever I pop in and see the dim glow of her android on the pillow, beside the pair of them. I will stride in, self-righteous as a tee-totaling preacher crashing an airport strip club, and launch into yet another litany of carcinogenic nightmares set loose by the mere proximity of a tiny device.

I feel like a dick. Maybe I *am* a dick. But then I think, *Better be a dick with a non-*

neuroblastoma suffering three-year-old, than a swell guy with a cancer tot. You've seen the cancer tots. Bald, feisty, dying. I don't know how people survive. The parents, I mean. The siblings. But I know—I feel—that survival would be made more hellish by knowledge that the torment was preventable. That the cancer was caused by what's the word, convenience?

Has my marriage suffered? Has my self-esteem nose-dived? Do I hate myself like a subway masturbator seeing his face flashed on page thirteen of every newspaper in America? Sort of, yes and yes. But—always the real shame—I can't stop! I see the phone, and even if it isn't on the pillow, even if it's on a table across the room, or in the closet, it doesn't matter. I know. The thing can be in a lead case secured by cast iron dipped in liquid steel, I'd just worry about the lead while worrying about the radiation. The grim sensation that I'm microwaving baby frontal lobe simply trumps everything else.

Phobic or diligent? You be the judge. All fodder to feed into the Daddy neurosis machine.

At least it keeps me from worrying about the pesticides in the water. Jeremy Fisher, in 2015, would likely have both male and female sexual organs. Among other mutations. Don't get me started.

#24
Tiny
Bran

dos

2 YEARS OLD

FORGIVE ME IF I'VE said it before, but now that I'm working dad duty without heroin I can see why I needed it. It's not just the pressure of dealing with the responsibility and commitment, it's the *never-endingness*. The specifics: like having to be at the pre-school at 4:15 to pick your toddler up and get her in the car and get home without smashing into a utility pole. And getting her in the carseat without pinching the flesh of her torso into some Social Services-worthy flesh wound.

And, question for study, am I alone with my obsesso car crash fantasies while muling my two-year-old through the streets of Los Angeles? The thing is, you can't space. Forget mindfulness. If I one-pointedly focus myself into the rear end of a Dodge Ram going eighty-five on the Hollywood Freeway, it's going to hurt as much as if I was texting and changing my playlist and talking to my hand agent. (Have I mentioned that I'm blessed with the hands of a Maine fisherman, and make a decent side living modeling them for moisturizer and tuna ads? Not important.)

Of course, even if we make it home, we're not safe. My house was apparently designed to kill children. This is evident at once by the sheer drop from the wooden deck to concrete and cactus below—easily accessed by any two-year-old with a will and a chair. And that's just the beginning. Instead of a backyard we have a thorny hill. Climbing up and down it are uneven wooden stairs, with great irregular gaps in between the steps, perfect for snapping a pre-three femur like a popsicle stick. I could go on, but you get the point.

Our house is toddler death trap, yet no one's ever come by to check it out. By contrast, I had to endure a thorough inspection from a sullen, judgmental woman named Hepler before I was allowed to come home with my first rescue dog, a six-year-old black chow-shepherd mix found tied to a parking meter on Skid Row. Thankfully, the Department of Parental Worthiness never showed up for a tour, so here we are.

• • •

AFTERTHOUGHT: CAN WE RETURN to the matter of texting and driving? Everyone reading this should stop immediately and hit Netflix to watch Werner Herzog's scarifying little doc on the subject, *From One Second To The Next.* It won't make you stop your drive-by typing, but at least you'll know how absolutely fucked the consequences of doing so are. You think you know what heartbreak and tragedy look like? Enjoy. Even if I'm not sporting a Baby on Board sticker in the back, I am, much to my own daily surprise, sporting a baby.

George Carlin called "Baby on Board" the three most puke-inducing words in the English language. And it's not like the stickers, started in 1984 by some marketing genius who deserves to be strangled, actually make a difference…Said genius, Michael Lerner, claims he invented them because he was driving his nephew around and cars were flying by so aggressively he thought the notice of precious life inside his death-box would slow things down. Of course it's stupid, but that doesn't mean Mr. Lerner can't now afford a private island crawling with babies who look just like him. Which reminds me, I once travelled to Tetiaroa, Marlon Brando's private Polynesian island, for a magazine story, and saw a dozen young, beautiful natives who sported the Godfather's face. And that was before I took the LSD. They really were his brood. This was, in fact, the last time I dropped acid, though the melting features of the little Brandogangers were less disconcerting than sitting at a group dinner and hearing Don Corleone, who ran the island as a resort for rich Europeans, complain about the price of New England butter.

My first and only chance to talk to the greatest actor of his generation, and New Zealand butter-thieving turned out to be pretty much the alpha-and-omega of his worldly concerns.

Then again, Brando had a lot of mouths to fill.

#25
Full-
Time

r

o Months Old

OKAY THEN. IT'S SOMETHING after 5:00 a.m. and the giant crazy-ass German Shepherd puppy and snotty senior basenji have been walked. N-tot and her mom remain unconscious. I'd say I've got some "me-time" but I'd have to spray Febreze in eyes right after typing it. So much shame! Where does it come from?

Time as a concept changes post late-game Dadhood and pre-death. Unless you've got a team of nannies and personal assistants—and if you do, God bless—time for both parents is pretty much constricted by that needy little dream-killer you've invited into your home. (Possibly the worst sentence I've ever written, but now it's 7:49 and my word count is at ninety-three.) I know I've got about fifteen minutes before my little girl wanders in and asks if she can watch *Maleficent*. We only let her watch movies with positive role models. And yes, as any parenting handbook will tell you, letting your thirty-monther start her day zoning in front of the big screen diddling her belly button and sucking on a fifth of rice milk is a sure way to guarantee future success and fulfillment.

Still, being a conscious (if easily pushed around) elder-parent, I try not to just give into movie demands immediately. Instead it's about reading books—is *The Little Engine That Could* ever more poignant than when an old man is reading it? Because she's a multi-tasker—and charter member of the FADDC, Future Attention Deficit Disorder Club—even when we're reading, we're doing something else. If I've sliced some apples and made some eggies for breakfast. (Yes, I am man enough to say "eggies." I don't give a fuck.) Finally she plops her thirty-month-old ass in the Distraction Chamber so we can watch *Coraline*, read *The Little Engine*, and eat those eggs and apples at the same time. Possibly while finger-painting and playing with dinosaurs. Call me demanding, but it's an early message the Stahl clan has been imparting for generations: anything worth doing is worth doing while eating, reading, and watching TV.

But wait—lets get back to nannies. Assistance. Au pairs. *Help.* A lovely and grotesquely successful actor I used to write with kept a wet-nurse, a day nanny, a night nanny, a sleep specialist, a baby chef (for when the kid got off the Brentwood teat and switched to solids), and an actual toddler trainer. Working those little baby abs so they'll be mini six packs by summer.

Truth be told, it's not even the minutes-and-seconds time you spend in babyland that drains you. It's the psychic time. The psycho-emotional hell hammer of What If…for which the actual child need not even be present. I'm talking about the you-could-get-a-call-any-minute-that-a-bus-jumped-the-curb-and-pancaked-your-child reality which people who don't have kids will never get. My pal Marc Maron has a great bit about talking to a married Dad who, between declarations of his absolute joy at being a husband and father, details the smothering, responsibility-laden hell he actually inhabits. After which he stops talking about itself long enough to ask Marc how *he's* doing, and Maron replies, "I'm great, I'm gonna leave here and go do whatever the fuck I want."

It's not that guys without children begin to seem like man-children to the jealous, self-righteous bastards who do have them. Or not just. Personally, I project onto kidless pals a freedom I actually did have for most of my life and didn't really exploit, beyond writing around the clock and spending an inordinate amount of time naked. Was I a damaged woman magnet? Did I write a batch of massively non-selling novels? Did I weird myself out of high-end Hollywood gigs by spending so much time alone when I finally had to have lunch with yak-faced studio execs to seal the deal I'd forgotten how to speak? Yes, yes, and yes.

Once my First Daughter was of age, I stopped worrying about the dailies. Not that I was there, in the earlier wilds of smack-fueled assholism, to do more than pick her up from school and play Uncle Wiggily. I was out of the house and holding down the corner of Crack and Eightball by the time she was two. Once the hands-on aspect went away I was free to waste my life, lose money, and destroy my liver unhampered by hard-core fatherhood.

What can I say? That white picket fence can be more exotic than all the fuckmeat and absinthe parties at Marilyn Manson's. (He said with trembling conviction.) On the other hand, I'm too old to be invited to Marilyn's, so what do I know? If you've lived long and abnormally enough, square really is the last frontier.

#26
Daddy
Has a
Clown

Little

Man

2 Years Old

WHAT CAN HAPPEN, WHEN you're shoveling in food with a toddler fork, is you start to feel like an angry, out-of-control giant.

This would be bad enough, by itself. But things get amped up when you've got a pint-sized life-cue sponge clocking you twenty-four-seven. Behavior which, pre-late life Dadhood, might have comprised some mildly shameful compulso activity become, post-daddydom, wildly significant. Now you're living with a creature whose whole mode of being is largely based on doing shit she sees you do. Which can be awkward when you're a pre-senior with questionable habits, and she's not even three.

"Oh I get it," you can hear her tiny hypo-thalamus saying to itself, "when I grow up, I'm supposed to stand nude in an open refrigerator and fork in dollops of sunflower butter. Ideally while pinching my temples with my non-spoon hand and spitting out the word fuck.

Fuck Fuck Fuck Fuck Fuck Fuck *Fuck!*

•   •   •

I HAVE NO ILLUSIONS, as parent (or humanoid) that I stand-out as some paragon of non-creepy, positive, and/or imitation-worthy living. Just the opposite. Things get wobbly, on the best of days. But I know, from my own long-ago childhood, how huge Dad's comportment looms in the Toddler Cosmos. My own father, when subjected to my mother's rage, would routinely put his head through a wall. She screamed insults, he head-banged, my sister cried, and I pretended it was all happening on an *I Love Lucy* episode. (My late mother, I should explain, wore the same up-swooped do as Lucille Ball, which may account for my misplaced sitcom identification.)

If you've never seen a grown man punch his forehead through plaster, no words can do descriptive justice. There's violence, and there's violence. But even as a tiny guy, I think I sensed that the real terror was going on *inside* the old man's head, and thrusting it through wallpaper roses was the only way he could MAKE IT STOP.

More than wall-banging, it was seeing my father nap facedown on the living room couch that really scared me. I always thought that he was dead. And would shake him mightily to make sure he hadn't morphed into a corpse. The poor guy couldn't get a break.

Pleased to report, the wall-holes were never plastered over, so that our little home came to resemble a diorama of Dad pain. Happily, I myself did not grow up to be a cranial wall-buster. Well, not often. I'm more of a puncher than a headbanger. Give me a brick wall and a brain full of hate and I'm good to go. Because, really, can anything beat the visceral thrill of leaving a restaurant-fight with your soon-to-be-ex and slamming your fist into the side of a post office? I like to think there's a rage-map of desiccated skin and knuckle-chunks all over lower Manhattan. Though, realistically, it's probably been covered up by the fist-blood of other relationship-challenged maniacs.

But back to fridge-binging. There's no way to know, at this point, if little NSS will grow up to be a loomer-before-leftover-and-condiment shelves. Among other things. I mean, I'm sure there are legions of enlightened men and women whose when-alone activities would do nothing to warp future grown-ups, should the little folk happen to be there as witness. Hard to find a single word to describe one's own personal history, but one that would not get the slot, in my case, is "exemplary."

Shit, as Dancin' Don Rumsfield used to say, happens. Take the other night, which happened to be New Years Eve. Because we are exciting swingers with a glittering social life, we were watching *Shrek* in what our little one refers to as the TV Room (not to be confused with the cross-dress friendliest bar in Dayton of the same name.) One thing led to another, and her mother and I found ourselves in the kitchen, naked from the waist down, doing a version of what the Animal Planet still calls copulating when sloths manage to it do without falling out of trees. A bit of private time in a day of forced— he said uncomplainingly—family togetherness.

At the key point in the proceedings—and why I suddenly sound like the narrator on the C-Span porn channel I couldn't say, except it's 10:00 a.m. and I've been up since 5:00 and my powers are waning—our child wandered in. Lately she's working a full-on Liza Minnelli. She struts into a room, flings her arms open wide and announces, as though stepping onstage at Carnegie Hall, "It's *ME!*" After which I scramble ankle-pantsed into the closet while my wife kneeled down and swooped her up in a giant hug. (That's two hugs in one sentence; my testicles have officially ascended to my lungs. I don't think I have ever written the word "hug" before, except once, when profiling the late Leo Buscaglia, aka Doctor Hug, in an eighties magazine profile. But it still curls my toes, for reasons either too obvious or too grim to go into. I'm just going to say "naked hugs" and "Mommy." Do the math.)

Ultimately, you just don't know what's going to imprint and fortify a future of self-loathing and Body Dysmorphic Disorder in your child. A couple beats after the whole hot kitchen action interruption, N asked, in that trying-to-figure-it-out-way kids have, "Mommy, were you helping Daddy make his pants happy?" How did she know?

While we're on the subject of tots glimping naked Daddy—no typo, I think glimp is a better word for an impressionable pre-three-year-old confronting paternal dangle—my take is: no big deal, but don't make it a habit. You don't want your kid to be the one who strips and belts out *Anaconda*—"I got a big fat ass!"—just like Nicki Minaj. That said, here's a fun family anecdote: the last time I took a bath with our child, she looked up as I clumped out of the tub and pointed, "Look, Daddy has a little clown-man!"

I thought of a million things to say. "Me and every other guy, honey." Or "That's what Mommy says." (I know enough comedians to know how to handle hecklers.) In the end I self-vetoed. Instead, I went with "How about I put your towel in the dryer, and make it toasty-woasty."

Maybe you have to be a little clown-man to understand.

#27
Juju

bes

AS AN OLDER FELLOW, you, the OG Dad, will have occasion to be surrounded by men half your age, with children the same age as your child. And possibly, wives the same age as your wife. I have a child the same age as the super-young wives, so it all works out.

No judgment, fellas, just the niggling awareness, when you're fumbling for small talk with the other parents in the parking lot after dropping your tykelet off, that you're an object, not just of curiosity but of conversation. (Awkward truth, you can't be my age and walk around with a cool, thirty-ish partner and not be used to the smirky, loaded glare of random age-appropriate dudes. Fact of life, cowboy. Remind yourself—if I may introduce a once-in-a-blue moon sports analogy—that Roger Clemens was striking out twenty-one-year-olds in his forties. A memory I dispense, despite the fact that, just this morning, I threw a rock at a telephone pole from ten feet away and felt my shoulder pop with such force I shrieked like a little girl, after which I had to strap on an ice pack and gobble Advil like jujubes to put a dent in the throb. Yes, Virginia, sometimes a man does miss opiates.

But wait. Dated-reference alert: do jujubes still exist? Excuse me while I Google. Apparently they've been around since the twenties, and are now available by sending off to OldTimeCandycom. Enough said. The other day I made a Larry Storch joke and no one knew what I was talking about it. I won't say this didn't sting, but really, folks, I grieve for Larry. Forrest Tucker's sidekick on *F Troop*? Anybody? (Another Larry, Larry Charles—fellow fifty-plusser—and I were lamenting the fact that we were running out of people who got our references. Writing something together, we realized that name checking Joe Besser was perhaps too arcane for anyone under the age of fifty who didn't zone half their youth away watching post-Curly *Three Stooges* episodes.

And yet, Larry Storch? I'm sorry, kids. I'm not letting go, he still deserves a legacy.

•   •   •

MOVING ON. WHAT SAY we plunge into the joy that is the kiddie birthday party? Way back, with my first child, in the full flower of celebrity-junkyhood, I would enter some upstanding family home and be instantly iced by the (understandably) protective mother. I could always tell the moms who'd seen me sweat through my poly-blend talking heroin on *Oprah*. Could feel their sense that there was something vaguely, or not so vaguely, unsavory about me. Fast forward, and decades later I'm still getting stink-eye at the Bouncy House. But for different reasons. This time, it's some Tiger Mom who senses there's something vaguely, or not so vaguely, unsavory about a man who might be called "Pops" in a forties musical attending her three-year-old's American Girl theme party. And I can't blame her. Or couldn't, if it weren't for the sad truth that I'm probably imagining all of this. My wife, who's constitutionally saner, insists it's all in my head. Making the inarguable point that, this being Los Angeles, people are so self-obsessed the last thing they're thinking about is anybody else. Unless it's somebody who can give them a job.

Strangely, I felt just as alienated at three-year-olds' birthday parties when I was three years old. I was that "sensitive" little boy who cried in front of the other children. I'd sit in the kitchen with the moms, eating cake under the table so I could look up their dresses at their fur-parts, as I imagined they were called when I began obsessing on them. At, coincidentally, around three.

Full creep disclosure: I used to crawl between the black-seamed stockinged gams of the Jewish ladies at my mother's bridge parties and stare up through the panty girdles at their little lady-beards. Panty girdles by the way, remain highly-charged fetishistic thrill candy in my erotic fantasies, despite the fact that no woman I've been with has worn one since high school.) Which brings up one of the many disturbo aspects of having a child.

Watching my offspring in her preschool years, I can't help but remember the twisted dimensions of my own post-toddler psyche. When I was four, my best friend Stinko and I used to give his sister Zagnut bars for yanking down her pants and peeing in front of us. Until the afternoon his older brother, Zeke (yes, there were Zekes in my neighborhood) caught us pee-gazing in the alley behind my house and hit us both with garbage can lids. Zeke ended up going to Vietnam and never coming back. But one thing he did in his short life was cure me of perving on friend's sisters. Which is no small thing.

Looking at children now, it's hard not to wonder, in an uncomfortable way, if the insane and retro-reprehensible shit that went on in my head when I was their age goes on in theirs. And then I think, they didn't have my mother. I'm sure they're fine.

Back to the hell-fest of kiddie birthday parties. My last took place at a house full of Silver Lake hipsters. Hoping to be "a part of," as they say in group, I chime in on the subject of Australian hiphop sensation Iggy Azalea. Mishearing her name, I refer to her as "Izzy", as if she supplemented her hiphop career moonlight as a kosher butcher. Not good. The Hipster Dads' smirks stayed hidden under their Castro beards. I kept my dignity in a sea of skinny jeans and Western-style plaid shirts. But I know, in my heart of hearts, that my own skinny jeans-wearing days are over. I never really wore them to begin with. And it's not like, in my post-fifties, I've Godzillad into some bloated pre-corpse. But still. Post-fifty skinny jeans = a cry for help.

Even at a beefy six foot, 193 pounds, with regular gym visits, I lately find myself staring at the locker room mirror and seeing a cream cheese sculpture staring back. No matter how much I lift weights, quiver through Chi Gong, or jog, I don't think those man handles are ever going away in my lifetime. (I think they're called man handles now; in my day—did I just say "in my day?" Jesus!—they were called love handles.) Along with Ms Azalea, I did not know who the Cold War Kids or The Birthday Boys were either. (And what's with giving yourself a name with "boys" or "kids" in it when you're a grown-ass man? Would the Marx Brothers be half as funny if they went with "Marx Boys?" Is it me? Is everybody just trying to hang on to their goofy adolescent dudehood?)

Whatever. In the Maron room, I hear about cool new bands and comics all day long. And still, all I can think is, *I'm all alone with my Larry Storch-love.*

The man was a genius. But I bet he was a strange little boy.

JERRY STAHL is the author of the bestselling memoir, *Permanent Midnight*, and seven novels, including *Happy Mutant Baby Pills* and *I, Fatty*. His widely anthologized fiction and nonfiction has appeared in *The Believer, Esquire, Black Book*, and a variety of other places. He currently writes for the IFC series *Maron*.